My Body's Callin'

Robin St.Clair

To Laurie
You are the Light
you seek! Creativity
shines in thrash and as
you! Love, Light & Peace
Robin St.Clair
2014

Published by:

TheRiteStep
Robin St. Clair
Brooklyn, New York 11236

Copyright © 2013 Robin St. Clair
Book Cover Illustration by: Reginald Butler
Book Cover and Editing by: Be Well Enterprises,
Corp. and Susan Andres, MEd

ISBN: 978-0-9898168-0-9
www.theritestep.com
Brooklyn, New York
Printed in the United States

Contents

Dedication

This book is dedicated to the following:

My maternal ancestors, the great mothers who came before me, whose shoulders I stand on, and whose legacies are rooted in love, nurturing, and authenticity:
Nanny (Celia Solomon)
Grandma St.Clair (Gertrude St.Clair)
Nana (Picola St.Clair)
You all continue to be the pillars of my growth and evolution.

Thank you for loving me unconditionally, Nana. You are my angel, my rock, and my blanket of comfort.

My mother, my greatest cheerleader and my best friend,
Sharon St.Clair.

My daughter, the sunshine of my life and the inspiration for my healing work and my ReBirth,
Brandi Shalia St.Clair-Edwards.

My niece, my other daughter and a beautiful demonstration of love, compassion and forgiveness,
Charon Chenelle Acevedo-St.Clair

and

My Body—my vow is to continue to love you unconditionally. Thank you for protecting me, nurturing me, and calling to me. I affirm you as healed, whole, and healthy.

My Body's Callin' for
Alignment with my Mind, my Spirit, and my
Emotions.

My Body's Callin' for
Love, attention, compassionate self-forgiveness, and
freedom.

My Body's Callin' for
Self-nurturing and to be acknowledged as Perfect
Health.

My Body's Callin' for
Healthy relationships, Reiki energy... *Rest.*

My Body's Callin' for
Enlightenment, Truth, Trust, and *Healing.*

Acknowledgments

Infinite gratitude to the Most High God!

God, I know you as Love, Light, and Infinite Peace. You are the answer to every prayer, every question, and every perceived obstacle. I could not have gotten this far without your grace and your mercy. God, I am so glad to know you. I'm grateful for your loving patience as I learned to move through resistance to accept *"the call."*

Thank you for the many manifestations of your love and compassion through the angels you've positioned on my path to teach lessons, share blessings, and love me through a process of self-discovery.

Thank you, God, for allowing me to experience countless incomplete cycles of action and many "do-overs." You've revealed yourself to me through faces, places, and experiences, and I am eternally grateful to you, because now, *I get it!*

I'm overwhelmed with joy by the circles of love and support you've placed on my path. With a heart of gratitude, I am honored to serve as a vessel of Love, Light, and Peace.

Inner Visions Institute for Spiritual Development (IVISD)

To the vision of my spiritual mother, Iyanla Vanzant, and the dedicated work of my entire IVISD family. Thank you for loving me, guiding me, and supporting me throughout my healing journey.

Thank you for teaching me to honor my feelings and identify pathologies and limited interpretations of reality. Thank you for nurturing my vision and teaching me to step out of the box of victimhood and despair to embrace my greatness. I've learned so much from you all, and I'm grateful to call you all family.

Thank you Reverend Lydia Ruiz for supporting me in identifying "the fight" and thank you Renee Kizer for supporting me in reconnecting to the *love*. Most of all, I thank you, Mama Iya, for seeing me beneath the surface and teaching me new ways of being. I learned the importance of moving back to get ahead through the process of introspection, prayer, meditation, and heartfelt intention.

The concept for this book was born at IVISD. Thank you for guiding me to heal my relationship with myself and for the universal principles, tools, skills, and techniques I've adapted and integrated into my life. Looking into the mirrors of my life proved effective and healing. I learned how to be true to myself and how to co-create my life masterfully with inner authority and compassionate self-forgiveness. My life's work is now dedicated to teaching others how to do the same. Through this process, I began to embrace a conscious connection to Spirit. I now know how to get to God in three seconds flat!

Momentum Education

To the vision of Robin Lynn and the dedicated work of Robinson Lynn and my entire Momentum Family. Thank you for the beautiful example and experience of what it means and looks like to contribute to the world. Thank you for reminding me that I matter and inspiring me toward this book's completion with love, support, and accountability.

I'm most grateful for the reminder that solid declaration and clear intention lead to desirable results. I've acquired a new family of love and support right in my backyard. I'm grateful for this process that allows me to align with my life's work, where I get to touch, move, and inspire others by establishing connections and contributing to the world with like-minded people.

Special thanks to LT93. You are my rock when I need grounding and my water when I need compassion and understanding. Thank you all for the reminder that I am a Powerful, Authentic, and Responsible Leader!

East Brooklyn Poets (E.B.P)

To the vision of Rhea Ummi Modeste and Tracy Jackson and my entire EBP Family. I am honored to be a member of this group of talent. As a member of EBP, I can enhance and cultivate myself through creative expression.

Our synergistic *FIYAH* keeps me inspired and connected to Spirit through my writing. Thanks for the continued reminder of the power and impact of the spoken word.

Spirit of a Woman (SOW) Leadership Development Institute

To the vision of Iya Monica Cherise Dennis and Iya Shawnee Renee Benton-Gibson and the entire SOW Village:

What a pleasure to serve! Thank you for allowing me to grow and share my gifts and talents with the SOW Village. This program has been instrumental in so many ways. As a self-affirmed

x

cycle-breaker, it was important for me to seek support in raising my daughter while I was in *"process"* at IVISD.

Thank you for nurturing, guiding, sharing, and loving Brandi (Lesedi) through the good times and the challenging times. Thank you for filling in for me and for filling the gaps of understanding when I didn't have the words to support my baby because I was stuck in the muck and mire of my own stuff.

The impact the SOW Rites of Passage Program has had on the growth and healing of my relationship with my daughter is immeasurable. We've adopted new family members in the SOW Village, and now, as an Iya (spiritual mother) in the program, I have the honor and privilege of supporting young girls and their families in moving through familial issues and creating new paradigms with intention and strengthened relationships.

Thank you for allowing me to be myself as I serve and embrace my power, purpose, and passion.

St. Paul Community Baptist Church

My journey began at St.Paul Community Baptist Church. I am forever grateful to "Church Unusual" for the lessons and blessings while on my quest to know God.

Reverend Johnny Ray Youngblood, you were instrumental in my mission to heal. Through the experience of The Maafa, I learned the concept and power of Sankofa. I thank you for your vision and for my first encounter with experiential learning through the Maafa experience. I've created loving connections and support circles that hold a special place in my heart.

Office of School Food

My first real job! I thank you for more than twenty-four years of experience. I've learned an effective formula for communication through my experience in labor relations. To the entire Labor Relations team (past and present), I thank you for your love, your support, and your understanding.

ReBirth Yourself Inaugural Group

To the ReBirth Yourself 2011-2012 Inaugural Group: Monica C. Dennis, Candice Watkins, Mama Sharon St.Clair, Mama Mut Ra-T, Laura Shmishkiss, Salema Davis, Nancy Butler, Debbie George, Leticia Bennett, Sheila Bennett, Charon Acevedo-St.Clair, Shannon Brown, Shalita Umpthery and Darlene Anderson. Thank you for trusting yourselves enough to trust God, but most of all, thank you for trusting me with your lives! Thank you for choosing *you*!

You've all done amazing work and continue to astound me with all you're up to in your lives.

Lifelong Friends

Each of you has greatly influenced my life. You've supported me through each cycle of my life. We've shared, laughed, cried, and grown together. Whether holding me accountable for what I said I would do, despite my whining *(to the point I wanted to punch you in the face)*, investing in me and holding my vision when I tried to run for the hills, making me laugh until I almost peed on myself, or lending me your shoulder to cry on, please know that, in your YOUnique ways, you are my rocks, my support, and my light.

I've been friends with some of you for more than thirty years! Thank you, Tracy K. Borden, Tanya Jones, Michelle Tillman, Antanell Robinson, Sandra D. Frayer, Sonia A.M. Daly, Tana Franklin, Melissa Beech, Kathi Thompson, Tina Guarino, Alicia (Subira) Hill, Lizelle Bissue, Lynn Horton, David & Danielle Wright, Troy Murchison, Michael Martin, Mut Ra-T and Charles (Carlos) Gordon.

Birthing Doulas

Without your loving support, suggestions, and feedback, I would still be in labor. Thank you for the push and the inspiration to keep moving forward. Thank you for the infinite ideas and creative suggestions for promoting this book. I love you!

Writing Coach/Editor, Self-Publishing Maven

Special thanks to Robin Devonish-Scott and your team of angels at Be Well Enterprises, Corporation and Susan Andres, MEd! Your guidance, support, and feedback were the *push* I needed to birth this baby and roll me out of the "delivery room." Thank you for seeing my vision and acknowledging that the birth of this project was so important to me. Your words, even when you had to yoke me with that sweet little voice and no nonsense attitude, were exactly what the Master Doctor ordered.

Family

Special thanks to my immediate family. I have such beautiful memories with each of you.

Mommy, Brandi and Charon, you all are my inspiration and motivation to stay *in action*. Poppy, words cannot explain my gratitude for all you do for me and the girls. Grandma Daisy, I love being your grandchild. Thank you for accepting me, loving me and letting me know that I matter.

Aunt Carol, you have such a huge and compassionate heart. Thank you for introducing me to creative expression through dance and recreational activities. Aunt Debbie, thank you for inspiring my spiritual and transformative journey. Uncle Jeffrey, thank you for being a blanket of trust and a cushion of paternal love that I could always confide in. Eddie, you are the best little brother anyone could ever have. I appreciate watching you mature throughout the years. Thank you for the beautiful gift of your children. I love them as if they were my own.

Thank you all for always having my back! Thank you for the memories, the inspiration, and the support. Thank you, family, for the *love*! I love you all!

Let the healing begin!

Introduction

These pages explore the depths of my soul. I learned from Iyanla Vanzant, a masterful and powerful teacher, that to understand something is to get beneath a thing at *its* core and *rise above it*.

Through my healing process of introspection and self-acceptance, I learned that to understand *it*, I had to look at *it* honestly, stand in *it* bravely, and accept the experience of *it* gratefully, before I could move through *it* or dismiss *it*.

What is *it*, you ask. *It* is victim consciousness, hurt, pain, anger, rage—the belief that I was unloved, unloving, and unlovable. *It* is the circumstance, the problem, the issue, and the consciousness that caused me to self-sabotage, self-loathe, and self-criticize. *You* name *it*.

I have been my worst critic. I could not understand why I had to experience pain in my life. I couldn't understand how God could be omnipresent and grant grace and mercy to those in need, yet *my* life had to be so *messed up*.

I lived in a self-created story of victimization. I was proud of my story too. I became a master at telling *it*—a master at *being it*. Unfortunately, I didn't know that what I did and the *way* I told the story were the things that kept me stuck. These stories were alive in my mind, yet they lay dormant in my body.

I felt unworthy, mentally cluttered, and emotionally traumatized, and I attracted the same experiences repeatedly—each time, expecting a different result.

The one thing that kept my sanity and supported me in identifying how I felt was my love for writing. Even as a small child, I used my life experiences as prompts to express my deepest feelings. It amazed me how I could create poems and short stories out of my pain. Sometimes, I chose to keep my poems a sacred secret— vowing that only God and I would ever know. At other times, I locked them away in the confines of boxes, storage bins, and journals I vowed never to reopen... until I realized the body of all my affairs called for love, freedom, rejuvenation, and healing.

Completing this book brought up a multitude of emotions. It has been one of the most challenging, scary, embarrassing, yet rewarding processes of my life. It took humility, vulnerability, compassionate self-forgiveness, and courage. I had to remind myself constantly of my intentions for this book. I changed the format at least three times. I finally chose to stay focused on the bigger picture—getting the *victim stories* out of my body.

It took a while, but I'm finally ready to stand in *my* truth. The following pages reveal the density of the stories my body had carried. Today is a new day! I no longer choose to allow the *its* in my life the negative power they once held. The *its* have become supportive tools and reminders of my transformation and my choice to *live*! Instead of being a servant to the *its*, they now serve *me*.

I intend to continue to *do my work* in identifying and releasing the disempowering *stories* that keep me stuck. My life consists of an integrated blend of prayer, self-affirmation, meditation, support circles, and constant self-reflection. I'm still on my healing journey, and I learn something new about myself daily.

I pray that you benefit from something in this book and learn to listen to *your* inner guidance so you, too, can transform your *its*, acknowledge your inner authority, and move forward in your life with power, purpose, and passion.

In Joy, Love, Light, and Peace,
  Robin St.Clair

Get Ready, Get Set, GROW

It hurt! One of the most painful events in my life was when he said, *"I'm not doing this anymore! I'm gonna end this! It's over!"* I blamed him for ruining my life. I blamed God for allowing such a thing to happen to me. I accused Love of being unfair. Love was gentle and kind to everyone, except me. What was I doing *wrong,* and why couldn't *I* get it *right?*

Have you ever loved someone or been *in love* with someone more than you love yourself? Have you ever felt that your life would end if you had to live one day without that person? Have you ever believed you found *"the one,"* your soul mate—that person who completes you and makes you "whole"? Has that person shown up in your life repeatedly in a different body with a different face? Could it be that you were in an insane cycle of being *in love* with the *thought* of the *feelings* of being in love? That's my story, and I basked in it for more than twenty years.

Sometimes, you can't see what you're doing. Sometimes, the answers come, but you don't even know that you've asked a question. You try to figure *it* out, only to be awakened to the harsh reality that you don't even know what *it* is or when *it* all started. All you know is your pain. All you know is your *story.*

I became a master at telling my story. I prided myself in my ability to re-create the story with imagery and dramatics while telling it to others. I wanted to be sure that they *got it*. Unfortunately, I didn't know that the constant reincarnation of my story was keeping me stuck.

I relived the story as I told it repeatedly... crying when necessary, laughing when appropriate, and cursing to add definition and impact. I often recalled the pain, but never accepted ownership or responsibility for myself. I wanted validation in my desire to be *right* about who *wronged* me.

I attracted the same experiences to myself over and over again. The answers showed up, but I didn't understand. It took me a while to *"inner-stand"* that I was the common denominator of each experience in my life. I finally accepted that, as a child, I might not have had power over my circumstances, but as an adult, I have the power to choose and to shift moment by moment.

For the sake of healing, I chose to identify with my story from a new perspective. I chose to tell the whole truth, even if it didn't make me look good or innocent or wise. I chose to rewrite the script of my life, and that's when I heard the voice of Spirit.

Fetch

I search in the closets of my heart and mind.
I'm amazed at the discoveries I continue to find.
As I carefully open one door at a time,
I'm attacked by the feelings I've learned to confine.

The first door I opened was Door #1.
I opened it up and remembered the fun.
I walked in a little farther on my tippy toes,
As a lovely aroma shot right up my nose.

It smelled like love... pure, whole, and sweet.
I closed my eyes, swung around, and landed firm on
both feet.
I took a deep breath and began to reminisce.
And for a hot, quick second, had an urge to tongue
kiss.

I took another deep breath, and I was wrapped in his
arms.
I severed the moment, and then heard the alarms.
What's buzzing and ringing and ruining my dream?
I paused for a moment at how real it all seemed.

I turned around to explore the commotion,
But something was triggered by a preconceived notion.
As I tried to stay snuggled and caressed in his grip,
The scenery around me fell down.
I tried to run, but I slipped!

4

"Oh, no," I thought. I want out of this dream.
This is the scene when I lose self-esteem.
I remember now—God get me outta here.
But God whispered to me saying,
                    "Fret not. I am here.

You asked me to show you what's blocking your
                    path.
This is an introspective journey—now buckle that
                    strap.
You need not ponder over what I reveal. The ultimate
                    goal is that you relearn to feel.

You've hid long enough and stifled your worth.
You forgot the anointing you've had since your birth.
Now that you are ready, I'll show you my dear,
How to step out of that box, as I draw you near.

These doors that fly open will only reveal
The feelings you've blocked and learned to conceal.
In order to continue on the path that is yours,
You must feel and experience what lies behind these
                    doors.

I know you can do it—I've prepared you for this day."

So, I took a deep breath and mustered some faith...

All right, God, I'm ready. Go on; show me the hurt.

God said,
"First things first—you must change your words.
Everything you've experienced in life was for good.
Your life has developed, as I knew it would.

You must ask for the lessons I want you to know.
All right, we'll just stay right here until you're ready
to go."

Oh, no, God, please... I can't stay here.
I'll change my words—look—Show me my fears.

What has blocked me on this journey called life?
Why do I sometimes feel alone and deprived?
What is it I tell myself right now and back then?
Why have I searched for love and acceptance from
men?

Why do I feel I need approval and protection?
Why do I yearn for reciprocity and affection?
Why can't you send me someone to love me for me?
Why do I feel some people are above me?

What have I done to deserve so much pain?
What can help me clear this emotional strain?
How many times will I open the same door,
Only to cry and fall on the floor?

I was here before, God. I just want to move on.
I don't want to go in; my heart feels so worn.

6

As I cried, and I wept, and I wept, and I cried,
God wrapped His arms around me, and I opened my
eyes.

Once I really stopped to see my surroundings,
I realized it wasn't all that bad, as I felt my heart
pounding.

It was beating again. I began to feel alive.
I was feeling again as God wiped my eyes.

In Search of Light

The more my soul questioned, the more the Universe presented me with experiences, challenges, and "work"—*inner work* that pushed me into self-reflection and accepting the truth of who I *really* am.

I prayed for more answers. I prayed for guidance. I prayed for God to show up and show out in my life. It was a simple consistent prayer, "God grant *me* mercy and grace. Let me know that I am not singled out, forgotten, unloved, or neglected." That's when my journey began!

I was guided to **"go back and fetch it!"** I literally had to revisit the issues, circumstances, and fallacies that kept me **stuck**. I had to go back to move through. I had to be in my body to awaken to the density of the pain I felt. It wasn't easy, but I learned that it is necessary and achievable.

I accepted my role as a student of Life. Master teachers appeared. They taught me the power of intention and living from the inside out. I learned to view my past as information, rather than another vise to kick my own ass. My teachers supported me in acknowledging generational patterns and pathologies. It all began to make sense to me.

Once I began to educate myself about myself, the labels of good/bad, right/wrong, and loyalty to everyone and everything but me became unnecessary. They, too, were constructs that kept me mired in the quicksand of the *victim story*. I began to forgive myself, which supported me in forgiving others. I began to acknowledge the divinity in myself, and I saw with my *Real Eyes*, that *I Am the Light I've been looking for.*

I'm a Cycle Breaker

I write to ignite the light that I shine;
Elevated consciousness dominates my mind.
Generational pathologies of lack and scarcity
Are transformed to abundance and prosperity.

Looking back at my past is a challenging task
But necessary knowledge to release this mask.
Transforming the story might seem absurd,
But it begins by the power in my words. ...

I'm Worthy! I'm Enough! I Can Do It! I Can!
I'm a Cycle Breaker, and I'm taking my stand.

For those who've gone on, and for those who stayed,
For those who stopped fighting, and for those who
prayed,
For those who have forgotten, and for those who stand
still,
I'm healing and transforming through the power of my
will.

It really doesn't matter how long it's takin'
'Cause through the power of my words, I know the
cycle is breakin'.

Family

Looking Back to Move Ahead

As I requested answers, I felt myself revert to my younger years. Why *was* I so angry? When *did* I conclude that I was unloved? What was my *first* experience in seeking love and attention from a man? Why *did* I feel I needed validation?

My introspective process began with a look at my relationships. I went back to the earliest memories of feeling unloved, unloving, and unlovable.

My biological dad was incarcerated my entire life. He and my mom were just sixteen years old when I was born. I knew who he was through stories—*other people's stories*. He was notorious, and people were afraid of him. I heard various stories from different people about respect, fear, admiration, and even hatred for him, but *I* didn't know him. I wanted to. I based what I knew about him on the stories I heard and the experience of *feeling* rejected and hated by my paternal grandmother. I saw her often as a young girl. She would look at me with piercing eyes and mumble something under her breath that didn't feel or sound good. She would cross the street when she saw me coming and call my mom a *black bitch* whenever she saw her. Perhaps it was never meant for me to hear, but I *did*.

My stepdad was physically present, but mentally and emotionally absent in my life. I yearned for acknowledgement, intimacy, affection, protection—some indication that I mattered to each father... but that wasn't my experience. I found some resolve in the fact that my stepdad's mom accepted me as her grandchild.

I experienced my maternal family as loving and nurturing, except for the times we disagreed. I recall hearing the traumatic stories of my grandmother and my mom feuding about my mom's pregnancy at such a young age. As the baby of the family, I was spoiled and the center of attention, even after my brother was born four years later. However, that attention did not discard the paternal attention for which I yearned.

I felt rejected, abandoned, and betrayed by my fathers. Perhaps that's when I created a story that I was unlovable, despite the evidence of love I experienced from my maternal family.

I was the apple of my Nana's eye! She co-parented with my mom, and what I didn't learn from my mom, I learned from my Nana. She was the matriarch of the St.Clair clan and instilled core values in us that carry her legacy to this day. She was my *everything*, and when she transitioned, it felt as if a part of me went with her.

I watched the women in my family bust their asses to "make things work" to hold the family down by any means necessary, so that's what I learned to do—stay busy, believing that true living is in the *doing*, not in the *being*. The *learned* behavior supported me in putting myself last on my list and negating my self-worth.

My perspective began to shift as I did my inner work. Although I felt the absence of love from my fathers, I remembered the love and nurturing I received from the men in my life. My grandfather, Poppy, is amazing! He loved to make me happy and see me smile. He was and is loving, gentle, kind, and giving.

I also received love and nurturing from my uncle, Jeffrey. Uncle Jeffrey taught me how to play tennis, how to drive, and he often took me to the park. I was his *Snoopy*. These men continue to be positive male role models in my life, and I love them. As generational patterns continue, their love is now equally poured into my daughter. She is the apple of Poppy's eye and Uncle Jeffrey's goddaughter. Unfortunately, like me, she, too, yearns for acceptance, love, attention, and affection from her father.

When I became a mother, I adapted a new posture. It was important for me to show my daughter and my niece, whom I raised from the age of two, that they matter. It was important for me to create joyful memories. I valued our family gatherings, but cringed when the children witnessed our family brawls. I thought I needed to protect them, but in hindsight, I acknowledge that I projected the thoughts and feelings of my inner child onto them.

I have an abundance of positive, loving memories from my childhood. I can honestly admit that I had *fun*! I was committed to offering a similar experience to the children in my family and their friends. My inner child had a ball in the process! I later learned that the time I spent nurturing the kids was yet another opportunity to avoid focusing within.

Nurturing my inner child was challenging at times, but through it all, I accept that the *big people* in my life did the best they could do. They were who they were because of who they learned to be. Once I became a parent, I appreciated my childhood in so many ways.

Daddy's Little Girl

I sit in my room with tears in my eyes.
I try to hold my tears back, but I want to cry.
Waiting for the day you will give me a hug;
Trying to be strong, but it's getting too rough.
Why is it that you don't have the time?
Why is it that when I see you, it's on your time—not
mine?
I invited you to all my shows.
You say you're coming, but you know you won't show.
I want you in my life;
I need you here.
Show me that you love me.
Show me that you care.
Is it asking too much to have you in my world?
Show a little bit of love.

Signed,
Daddy's Little Girl

I Ain't Mad No More...

I ain't mad no more
'cause the paternal nurturing I didn't get from you,
came to me through the grace of God.

When I needed a father to make the image of my
family complete, I saw my stepfather.

I ain't mad no more
'cause I have memories of sitting on a lap, driving a
car, and Father's Day cards that I made for my
Poppy—not you.

I ain't mad no more
'cause when I wanted to go to the park, spend quality
time, and learn to drive, my uncle was there.

No, I ain't mad no more
'cause I made it—without you.

The thought of you has consumed my being for too
long.

I yearned for you, but you ignored my needs. You
blamed everyone under the sun for the demise of our
relationship when I was little.

Daddy, what's your excuse now?

17

I ain't mad no more.
'cause God blessed me with father-figures and male
role models that give me wisdom, nurturing, love, and
care... and I love them.
But, Daddy...

I Wanted You!

I Needed You!

I wanted to love *you*, too, Daddy!

I—am—not—mad—at—you—anymore...

Or am I?

My Mom, My Friend

You were just sixteen when I was born.
You fought with your mom—This Baby Was Yours!
You wanted someone to love who would love you the
same.
Nana gave in, even gave me my name. ...
Although you were young, you had principles instilled
That kept you focused and very strong-willed.
Four years later, my brother came.
I thought things would be different, but they stayed
the same—
A loving mom, a loyal mom, a gentle mom, a royal
mom.

I was four or five when we had our first talk.
I remember so well because Eddie couldn't walk.
You sat me down for our first session—
Our bonding talks and my valuable lessons.

Lesson #1—Them Good for Nothin' Men
"You're too good for that, Robin;
They'll leave you sobbin'.
They're nothing but trouble,
Create too many problems.
They'll boost you up, and then bring you down.
Have self-respect, accept nothing from those clowns.
You can do bad all by yourself,
So carry this with you.
Lord, I hope it helps!"

19

Lesson #2—Get a Good Education
"All I ask is that you finish school.
Be the best you can be 'cause I ain't raised no fools.
You've got a good head on your shoulders, so use it
wisely.
Don't let peer pressure become too compromising.
Don't listen to your friends—you listen to me.
You'll thank me later. You watch—you'll see."
I can go on and on with the lessons I've been taught,
But there's not enough paper for all my thoughts.
I will summarize it all by letting you know
That, Mommy, my friend, I love you so.

You have taught me life's lessons.
You have listened to my grief.
You were there when I cried, and you rocked me to
sleep.
A shoulder to cry on—I always had yours.
Friends came and left, but you I adore.
My friends would envy the bond we shared.
They came to you with their problems—You showed
them you cared.

I became an adult, what a journey we traveled.
The mysteries, the lessons, all begin to unravel.
Just listening before, my ears and your face,
It all makes sense now—it falls into place.
With all the warnings, with all those talks,
I still had to fall before I walked.
You created a cushion, so it wasn't so hard.

You allowed me to fall but nursed my scars.

You were my support during the birth of my child.
Although it was hard, you made it seem mild.
I was scared as hell—they called you at work.
I was crying for my mommy like a little jerk.
You met me at the hospital; you ran up the stairs.
You came in the room and wiped all my tears.
"It's ok, Robin, now I'm here.
No time for crying, no time for fears.
In a couple of hours, you'll be somebody's mother.
You'll be smiling then, and I know that you'll love her."

I have to stop now, but, Mommy, you know
That words don't express how I love you so. ...

Motherly Speaking...

*As a mother, I am blessed with the gift of being my
child's first teacher, nurturer, and guide.
As a mother, I feel joy each day I gaze into my child's
eyes and embrace the beauty and divinity of her soul.
As a mother, I am to my child as a lioness is to her
cub.
It is my God-given duty to see to it that my child is
clear of danger or harm.*

*When my child faces the challenges of life, I feel her
pain.
When my child excels in school, I share her
enthusiasm and joy.
As a mother, I embrace not only my child, but every
child I encounter, for they are my children too.
It is my motherly duty to spread love, shine light, and
promote peace in my household and everywhere I go.
As a mother, I acknowledge that my child is God's
child first.
It's not always easy embracing that, as a mother, there
are times I must let my child fall to get up.
As a mother, I am learning how to respond, rather
than react.
I am learning with my child as I teach my child.*

*As a mother, I serve in many capacities—from
nurturer to guide and disciplinarian to teacher.*

22

From "You just don't understand, Mommy!" to "I'm not you!"
As a mother, I acknowledge that the question beneath the statement is
"Mommy can you help me inner-stand?"

As a mother, I embrace the spirit of the lioness.
I contribute to the family and the community's wellbeing.
I take pride in my family and thank the ancestors for paving the way.
I teach my child to do the same.
My role is to strengthen and nourish my mind, body, and spirit and seek guidance from the Most High God.

As a mother, I must lead by example and be the example I want to see in my child and in the world.
It's a challenging role; however, I am grateful.
I accept, and I am joy-filled to be Brandi and Charon's mother.

Motherly Speaking

23

I Thought You'd Live Forever

I thought you'd live forever
Could I have been wrong?
I thought you'd live forever.
Did you die? Should I mourn?

I need to take a minute—to sit and to think...
Of how it all happened so fast—
Seems all I did was blink.
You've shown me your love.
You've taught me so much.
Now, all I long for is your gentle touch.

I thought you'd live forever.
You never said that you would.
You were so strong and so caring.
I just thought that you could.

You gave me advice. You said, "No, that's not right!"
I was stubborn and bratty, but I still saw the light.
I would call you later to apologize.
I said, "Nana, I'm sorry—now, I realize...
Your age and experience are what make you so wise."
Never once did you say, "You think you're so smart."
You just showed sincere love from the depths of your
heart.

I thought you'd live forever.
Your body will be missed.
24

I can't end it now—there's more to reminisce...
I remember the time when your hair turned gray.
I asked, "Nana, are you gonna die?" Then, you turned
away.
You spoke soft words and turned back around.
You said, "No, Boogs, I'm not."
The next day, your hair was brown.
Little things like that—you did only for me
To make me feel special—to pacify me.

I thought you'd live forever.
This is gonna be hard.
I looked through your things;
I found all my cards.

Through the years, I tried to tell you how much I love
you.
Through the years, I tried to tell you—but I know that
you knew.
I couldn't believe it,
Every last one,
From summer camp to college—the hard times, the
fun....

As I reread those cards, I began to see
That you will live forever, Nana,

Because You Live in Me

Nana Didn't See the Tree

*You might have thought your efforts were washed
right down the drain,
But I remember the lectures, Nana;
You did not speak in vain.
You probably thought no one listened, but your face
would say it all.
I heard the expression on your face when we had our
family brawls.
Our family's roots were planted on the foundation of
Love,
Intertwined in Faith—like a hand in a glove.
There's no need to worry, and there is no need to fear.
The branches have already sprouted; the leaves have
now appeared.
Four generations were born of this tree.
You thought it wouldn't grow.
I know from where you sit, Grandmother, you're
smiling down below.
You might not have seen the tree grow
When you were on this plane,
But I know you know it's growing now;
Your work was not in vain.
We still need you, Nana.
I know you hear my cries.
If God will let you intercede, then please help us
release the lies.
Four generations are enough to support and grow this
family tree.*

26

I want to be to my grandkids what you have been to
me.
If God will let you intercede, I request you shine your
light.
Please guide us out of darkness
So we can release the fight.
Please watch over Brandi, and shine light on her path
too.
If God says yes—and I know God will, please help me
stand in Truth.
Nana might not have been able to see the tree,
Yet Nana lives within it.
God's blessed our family with her light.
We all embrace her Spirit.

The Unbroken Chain

*When my Nana was alive, I took life for granted. My
grandmother was the matriarch of my family.
She was known for instilling family values, being
straightforward and strict. But most of all for her
sharp tongue—she'd tell you off so quick!*

*You'd sit there for a minute thinking about what you
did,
And then, you'd sigh in bewilderment, feeling a little
stupid.*

*Her affection and love pierced through your soul.
You'd want to be angry with her, but you'd just let it
go.*

*Nana held the family together like Elmer's glue.
She would run down the "you betta nots" and the "you
betta not dos."*

*She was well respected at home, on the job and in the
community as well.
But don't get me wrong; piss Nana off, and the whole
block heard her yell.*

*She'd tell you what you did wrong and tell you where
to go.
Yet she'd praise you when you did well and brag to her
friends about how much you know.*

28

Reminiscing about Nana makes me realize that the
chain is not broken because, still, we rise.

Nana is now an ancestor—we're no longer a
generation of four.
I'm all cried out! I can't cry anymore.

Heaven sent angels down and gave Nana her wings.
Knowing this and experiencing her love—I can't
explain the joy this brings.

Mommy and Brandi, we're now a generation of three.
I need you both in my life, and I hope you two need me.

When I look at you, Mommy, I see more than my
mother.
I see a friend, a confidante, and I know there could be
no other.

Mommy, you know me so very well.
You know what's in my heart.
You cry when I cry; you laugh when I laugh.
But that's not all, Mommy—that's not even the half.

You were my support during the birth of my child.
Although it felt uncomfortable, you made it seem mild.

Brandi, I love you—my other best friend. I want us to
create a bond that will never ever end.

Nana's love and affection have now trickled down to me.
This chain is unbreakable, and I intend to make you see.

My beautiful daughter, Brandi, you make me so proud
With your little squeaky voice that at times can seem so loud.

I pray that we can be as close as the generations before us.
I pray that we continue to laugh and have things to discuss.

I want to be the mom to you that my mom was to me
and her mom was to her. I want our love to grow and grow and never ever sever.

I will continue to hold these thoughts and prayers as valued tokens.
Because on Earth or in Heaven, the chain remains unbroken....

Before It's Too Late

This poem is dedicated to my mother, my mother's mother, and my mother's mother's mother. I dedicate this poem to my daughter, my daughter's daughter, and my daughter's daughter's daughter. This poem is dedicated to every woman whose mother has gone home. It is dedicated to any woman who has ever experienced conflict or dis-ease in her relationship with her mother.

This poem is dedicated to those who have chosen to forgive and those who refuse to forgive. This poem is dedicated to the powerful, exuberant, nurturing, phenomenal women in my family—five generations past and five generations to come. I dedicate this poem to those who have yet to pick up the phone, refuse to apologize, choose to experience pain and dis-ease in their relationships and to those who are ready to do a new thing...

Before It's Too Late...

31

Before it's too late,
I want to tell you that I love you.
I want to share my joy with you and celebrate together.

Before it's too late,
I want to tell you how grateful I am to have you in my life.
I want to tell you that no one can ever take your place because no one knows me as you do.
You know my secrets. You know my flaws. You know that part of me that needs to grow and the parts of me that have grown and matured.

Before it's too late,
Let me thank you for allowing me to fall and helping me get up.
You've taught me life's lessons by allowing me to have my experience of life, and when I made mistakes, you supported me and corrected me with love, compassion, and affection.

Before it's too late,
Let me tell you that I enjoy being in your presence, not because of who you are to me, but because of how I feel knowing that I am a product of your existence.
I respect you for your courage and your strength.
I respect you for the wisdom you share and the way you unregrettably share the stories of your past to the depth of your knowing.

32

Thank you for sharing your lessons. Thank you for sharing your pain. Thank you for admitting your brokenness and your desire to experience unconditional love, even when you are not aware of what you are doing.

I love you because you are an expression of God's Love. You never tell me who I am not; instead, you tell me who I am and whose I am.
You believe in me when I don't believe in myself, and you encourage me when I claim that I am in darkness.

Our relationship is sacred. You are my friend, my confidante, my nurturer, and my shield.
You are the pillow I lay on when I need a soft place to land.

Before it's too late,
I want to thank you for being my greatest cheerleader!
Thank you for being by my side when I gave birth to my daughter.
You held my hand as you always do. You stroked my head and told me everything would be OK.
Because I trust you, I believed you, and you continue to be a blessing when I need you.

Before it's too late,
I want to tell you how it pains my heart when we disagree.

33

I want to tell you how heavy I feel when the woman in me meets the woman in you, and our humanness is expressed in ways that, at times, depict two little girls in a battle competing to be heard.

Those times don't feel loving. We are caught up in the moment, and the words that land create feelings of inadequacy and lack.

We come from a long line of strong women... a long line of women who held on to anger, pain, hurt, and dis-ease.
We come from generations of doing-ness and unworthiness, and before it's too late,
I want to remind you that we have the power to break the cycle.

Before it's too late,
I want you to know that you are and have always been a terrific Mother.
You are and have always been someone I admire and look up to.
I strive to be the mother to my offspring that you are to me.
I strive to correct my flaws, share with my children, heal internally, and co-create from a place of power.

You've taught me to value life. You've taught me to value love. You've taught me to fight for what I believe

*in, and now that I am grown, I've learned that what I
believe in is worth the fight.*

*So, I fight my negative ego and trust that our
relationship is healed, whole, and healthy.
I fight procrastination and fear and move beyond the
adverse manifestations of my challenges and Empower
myself to move from victimhood to* victory.

Before it's too late,
*I want to tell you that I cherish nothing more than the
love of my family, except my friendship with you.
I want to tell you that, as the matriarch of my
immediate family, you are the epitome of a loving
mother and the "stuff" of your past is no comparison
to the gift of being* present.
*I want to tell you, dear mother that your labor has not
been in vain.
I want to remind you that you are* loved, loving, and
lovable.

Before it's too late,
Allow me to remind you of God's infinite love.
I invite you to share with me in my newfound state of
forgiveness, *because I've learned that when I am in
this state, I am* **Free of** *Guilt,* **Illness,** *Victimhood,
Envy, Negative* **Ego** *& Self Sabotage*™.

Before, it's too late,
Mommy, I want to tell you that it's never too late to
say
I love you!

By the Pool

It's summertime now.
How do I know?
The pool is open—the kids scream, "Let's go!"
By the poolside, I sit and observe.
The kids run out—they splash me,
The Nerve!
They're screaming and shouting Marco Polo with glee.
By the poolside, this is what I see.
The laughter gets louder.
The screams pierce through my soul.
God's little children are now on a roll.
As I sit by the poolside, I reminisce my youth;
It wasn't that long ago to tell you the truth.

I remember the hydrant, the pool, and the beach.
I remember the lectures and that parental speech,

"Don't stay in the water all day long—you'll get sick!
Don't do that handstand or any other tricks!
Stay where I can see you. Don't you go too far!
That hydrant is dangerous—watch out for cars!
Put that girl down—she must weigh a ton!
Now, go on back in—and—oh, yeah—Have Fun!"
With all the don't's, we still had a ball.
The limitations seemed small—didn't matter at all.

As I slowly come back to reality,
I watch the kids swim and tease playfully.

The sun's going down. I yell, "It's time to go!"
I scream, "C'mon y'all!"
They scream back, "Nooo!"
They ask for more time and begin to pout.
I stomp over to the pool...
"I said get out!"

As I leaned over to scold them with one last yell,
I lost my balance, and then I fell.

At first, there was silence—no laughter at all.
Then, I chuckled to myself and asked, "Lord, how did I
fall?"
The kids started laughing—then I broke my smile.
One grabbed a towel—the other stood there for a
while.
They straightened their faces and got ready to go.
Then, I screamed, "Marco!"
They screamed, "Polo!"

Butt, I Love You!

That's My Story, and It's Sticking to Me

In Search of Love

I'm pleased that I know, feel, and I have experienced unconditional love from my family. However, when I didn't get the paternal response I desired, I defaulted to the attention I received from boys.

I *thought* I knew what I wanted, but had no foundation to identify or define what I was experiencing from the guys I met. I knew what I didn't want to feel, but had no premise to articulate the experience I wanted in a relationship. I knew I wanted to feel loved. Unfortunately, I didn't know what that really meant. I held the thoughts of what I didn't want in my consciousness, and that is exactly what I experienced.

I had three *significant* intimate relationships. This is not to say that I've only dated three men. I simply acknowledge that three different men have made a major impact on my life. They became my *teachers*; however, none of us knew at the time that Life was in session. These three relationships educated me on the true meaning of love.

I experienced my first *love lesson* between the ages of twelve and fourteen with *Him #1*. My second *love lesson* lasted between the ages of fifteen and thirty-four with *Him #2*. The third experience of what

I *thought* was love with *Him#3* overlapped my experience with *Him#2* and lasted from the ages of twenty-one to thirty-one. There were times that I felt loved and validated by each throughout each relationship. I equated sex with love because it was the closest reference I had to the intimacy and paternal acceptance for which I yearned.

I accepted behaviors that devalued my worth. I participated in and tolerated actions that had adverse impact on my mind, body, spirit, and emotions. I idolized the *Hims* in my life because I was in search of *love*, and I convinced myself that they had what I sought.

****

The beginning of each relationship was nice. Those butterfly sensations surfaced. We exchanged terms of endearment such as Baby, Sweetie, and Boo with melodic adoration. A sense of ownership came over us because we realized that a strong bond began to seal the two of us together. As much as I tried to resist, I realized I was *open*!

Open

What is this feeling coming over me?
I'm at a stage in my life that holds no space for another,
Trying to be a strong, independent woman and hold it down as a single mother.

I try desperately to camouflage the smile beginning to surface when you enter the room,
Impressed with your intellect and dialect and your abundance of respect for a Real Woman.

I'm trying to ignore the touch of your hands when you try to get my attention
And trying not to let you notice the apprehension I feel
When you smile at me with that affirmative "gotcha" look on your face.

Arrogantly you stride past me, touching my shoulder
blade and glancing back
To make sure I felt your affectionate attack—
And I did 'cause...

The child in me dances gleefully as I turn and
reluctantly walk away with a face like
pa—lease!

And I know I'm just being a tease...

'cause I saw the bulge in your pants as my nipples
began to dance...

But this is business, not pleasure... so this feeling won't
be measured.

Once I realized I was open, I experienced all kinds of sensations. I wasn't sure if he felt it, but his words, attention, and the way he looked at me were validation enough for me. I wondered if he felt the vibe...

Vibin'

You feelin' me?
Cause I'm feelin' you...
The way you express yourself
The things you do....

You diggin' me?
Cause I'm diggin' you...
The gradual link of compatibility,

The entwine of minds and feelings of apprehension,
The conversation and concentration,
The hesitation and sweet sensation,
That ultimately lead to romantic temptation.

It makes me open and brightens my day!

You feelin' me?
Cause I'm feelin' you....

It felt as if some people I met were just playing mind games. Some of them just wanted sex. Others just wanted to screw my mind. I was tired of playing that game. My feelings were getting hurt. I positioned myself in defense mode, expecting to be rejected, abandoned, or betrayed. I began to approach all the guys I met with a shield of armor because I felt I had to prove I was not "stupid." I became a willing participant in a game of Mental Masturbation.

Masturbation of the Mind

Tease me first by staring into my eyes for a clue.
Anticipate my potential while congenially challenging my every move.
It's a game at first, but it quickly becomes personal to me.
Analyze and evaluate the situation at hand.

While countering your direct attempts to manipulate my mind, I size you up as well.

This game of tit for tat continues, as our minds are provoked to entwine
In this battle we feel is so divine.

*Masturbation of the minds suddenly combines to form
the kind of mind manipulation that causes frustration
because the duration of when to speak and the
temptation of what to say are wrongfully portrayed as
intimidation and degradation.*

And that is not the case.

*Your arrogance surfaces as my barricades shield me,
anticipating your next deliberate attack.
Like a knight with armor or a soldier on the battlefield,
I position myself in defense mode.
Arriving at my destination requires much thought and
concentration.
Quick answers would be the expectation, but I'm full
of hesitation because I know when I come,*

I gotta come correct.

*So, the combination of my motivation and explanation
shows the desperation
To prove I'm not a chicken head cluck cluckin'—I've
had an education.*

*I'm intimidated by your words, yet they stimulate my
mind.
Your words make me think, and then I feel inclined
To prove that a good debate and good conversation
Is really all we need in today's civilization.*

46

When we share with compassion and wisdom when we speak,
We raise the vibration of Love and become the epitome of what we preach.

A good debate begins first in the mind.
Now, masturbate on that and leave the negative connotations behind.

"You Love Me...Right?"

I met *Him #1* when I was twelve. By thirteen, he had cheated on me three times with three different girls. I knew, but I stayed anyway—because I thought I *loved* him. I had little temper tantrums and drama moments. We had physical disagreements. *Ahem...*we had fights! It all seemed normal to me. I watched my mom and stepfather fight and then get all *lovey-dovey*. I thought that was just what couples did. I stayed—because I *loved* him.

He told me *"everyone"* was doing it. He told me that girls were knocking down his door to *give* him some and that I should stop "holding out." After all, he was one of the cutest guys in the projects (at least I thought so). I felt *lucky* to be with him.

"If you love me, you'll do it. Lemme be the one to bust your cherry." Things would be going fine. I'd be feeling good, and he'd go and ruin the mood, pressuring me to have sex with him so he could be my "first." It was two years from the date he asked me to go out with him. I didn't feel prepared. He said that two years was enough preparation. *"You love me—right?"* I would answer with a weak, "You know I do, but..." He would cut me off mid-sentence and say mockingly, *"But, I'm not ready?"* I quickly learned how to play the game and responded to that, "And if **you** love me like you say you do, you will wait until *I*

48

am ready." That shut his ass up for a while. Just a little while...

I wanted him to understand. I didn't want to lose him. He knew just what to do to make me feel *good*. Even though I was afraid and really wanted to wait, I did *it*—because I *loved* him. I experienced a major shift in my life at the age of fourteen. I was no longer a virgin. We did *it* more and more, which in my mind meant he really loved me as much as I loved him. It didn't matter that one leg of my pants would be on and the other would be off or that my shirt was half choking the shit out of me because it was rolled above my breasts. We were *doing it*. I disregarded the way he would jump up, put his clothes on, and leave me sitting there half-butt-assed-naked, half-clothed. He said he didn't want my mother to come in and "bust" us. I felt nasty the first couple of times, but after a while, I just dismissed the feelings of unworthiness, insecurity and abandonment as "freaky" and greedy—because that's what *he* said it was. By this time, I believed I was *in love* and felt a tingly flicker in my body every time I thought of him.

I discovered that he was cheating on me again. This time, it started to hurt. I felt invalidated because I had finally given *it* up to him, and the thought that he was getting *it* from someone else made me sick to my stomach. The bad feelings outweighed the good

49

feelings because while he was "out there," I was at home, feeling miserable, depressed, and unwanted. I felt abandoned and unloved at the age of fourteen. I started to believe he didn't deserve to be with me, but some of my friends told me I was stupid even to think about letting him go, so I stayed—because I *loved* him. I didn't want to risk the chance of any *triflin' chicks* stealing "my man."

After he cheated a few more times, I was done with his shit and ended the relationship. I didn't care what anyone said. I was back!

Him imposters showed up throughout the year. They had some of his characteristics. Sometimes, I felt good in my body when the imposters were around, but I wrote the feelings off, declaring, "*Nah...that's not it, and he is* not *him!*" At times, one date was all it took for me to see right through the imposter. He only wanted one thing, and I was not about to give *it* up to *him*—not with his "imposter ass," anyway. When was the *real Him* going to show up?

He finally showed up in all his *Him* splendor in a different body with a different face when I was fifteen. Because his physical appearance was different, I thought everything about him would be different.

50

Him #2 and I had fun. We finished each other's sentences. We laughed. We shared. We were compatible, and I called him my soul mate. I enjoyed being with him. Most of all, sex with Him #2 was adventurous. The first three years were blissful. We were together all the time. We talked about being together forever, and although I stayed committed to the thought, he changed his plans, but I didn't get the memo.

To Be Loved by You

To be loved by you meant so many things;
I still can't explain the joy it brings.
Being in love with you controlled my heart,
And I knew I was in love with you from the start.

I once thought being loved by you was nothing but a joke
Because the day love stepped out on me was the day my heart broke.
I loved you, and I trusted you more than you'll ever know,
And I guess that's why it's still quite hard to release and let it go.

I know; I know... you're sorry. Time moved on
We're different people now.
I'll forgive you and learn to love myself.
I know I will somehow.

51

But our bond was strong—I loved you;
I wanted to be your wife.
To be loved by you is what I wanted for the rest of my
life.

Identifying sex as love was not serving me. I experienced confusion and pain on many levels, but ultimately allowed myself to become a human doormat! I allowed Him #2 to come and go as he pleased. I willingly gave him the key to my heart...

The Key

Our bodies would entwine in rapture so divine.
The touch and the feel of your flesh and mine,
The caress of your touch—that look on your face,
The careful way you went down, putting your face in its place.

The chemistry we shared was some real serious shit.

Wait...

Face still in place—sucking on the clit...

The thought of you right now is making me wet
'cause you have a Love Jones I'll never forget.

I want to touch your body and explore you from head to toe.
Then, I want to caress your manhood and never let it go.
I'll lick you and suck you on your neck and your back,
Then turn around—ass out—for the

Doggie Style Attack

Thrusting and pushing, moaning and groaning,
High from your love—I'm in my zone and
As I climax and remember the way it was before,
I remember that your lovin' kept me yearning for
more.

Your lovin' made me feel like the queen I am.
Your lovin' made me think you would always be my
man.
Your lovin' I missed when you chose to depart.
You turned the lock with your key, but

I Padlocked My Heart.

Trying to ignore the feelings and sensations that arose didn't work for me. When I'm in, I'm in! I shared my inner feelings and most sacred desires with Him #2. I allowed myself to be vulnerable enough to be seen. I gave 100 percent of myself and didn't always experience reciprocity. The pain and the anger grew, but I hadn't realized it. I numbed my emotions, ignored my intuition, and began to abandon myself. If only he knew...

Only You...

Only you knew what lay beneath the surface.
Only you knew the scars that blemished me.
I did not share myself with anyone else, but you—I was committed to you.

You unzipped the protective layer and saw deep into my soul.
Only you pinpointed my ups and downs.
Only you heard the inner sounds of my heart and my mind—my eyes and my face.
Only you made my juices boil and my heart begin to race.

I searched over and abroad for the type of love we shared.
I searched high and low, but no other love compared.
I kept searching for the love we lost,

But time after time, I got lost in the sauce.
Hurt after hurt and pain after pain,
I learned to protect myself from the emotional strain.

Always referring to the love I once had,
Yet wanted to hate the lover that made me so sad.
Hurt turned to anger—the demise of my soul.
Only you saw my inner light—
You knew me when I felt whole.

For twenty years, I salvaged the thoughts,
From tenth grade to college—childhood to adult.
We grew apart—that was the result.
Sadness to resentment,
A hurt like that bore no name.
I wonder how you would have felt if you endured the
same.

Only you could imagine how hard it was for me,
To dim my light and stuff my pain, ignore my
sensuality.
To not want to be touched and deny another's
affection,
To reject another's manhood and rebuke his erection.

Only you took me on a mental journey of joy,
Fantasizing it was you when it was my sexual toys.
Reminiscing the feel of your tongue on my clit,
Sucking my breast and fondling it.

Only you made me climax
One time, two times, three times... four
Only you had me climbing walls and screaming out
more!

Squeezing your butt cheeks and scratching your back,
Legs on your torso—face in the pillow,
Stroking it rough—then taking it
Slo-o-ow.

Only you can bring me joy and then sorrow,
When I think about you again tomorrow.

The years flew by, but padlocking my heart didn't stop him from coming back. He just kept using his key, so I let my guards down and tried to be his "friend." I rationalized that we had gone through so much together. At the very least, I honored his request to spend time with me... *for old time's sake.*

Padlock

The game of love has no rules.
The players are wounded but try to play it cool,
Trying to win, and not be the fool.
Playing the love game sends your ass back to school.
I played the game, but I didn't win.
I played the game, and it hurt within.
I tried to toss the game to the side
Because my true feelings, I tried to hide.

I padlocked my heart and buried the pain.
I protected myself from the mental strain.
I became the best playa I could be,
And maybe that's why you're here with me.

You've taught me well;
My game is tight.
I bet you're thinking, "It's on tonight."
My sexy body got your tongue on the floor,
Yearning and beggin' and pleadin' for more.
I'll tease you with a kiss and fondle your tool,
Then watch as it grows as you suck in the drool.

Don't get too excited 'cause it ain't over yet.
I'm gonna make this a night you'll never forget.
Butt-ass naked—clothes thrown about,
You thought I would scream, but instead I heard you shout.
My titty, your mouth—your dick in my hand,
Why you shakin', baby? I heard you da man....

By the time foreplay's over, you're hard as rock.
I open up for you to enter...

Oh, baby, you forgot?

Ain't nuttin' happenin' tonight 'cause my shit is Padlocked.

I tried to stay true to myself, but eventually I gave in. I knew I was dishonoring myself, but I didn't know how to let go. While away at school, things seemed different. I felt it in my gut, but I couldn't quite explain the feeling, so I tried to ignore it. Focusing so much on Him #2 affected my studies, and I kept my dreams and aspirations on the back burner. I betrayed myself and held on to the fear of being abandoned by him, resulting in my abandoning myself. I gained weight. I felt heavy. Instead of weighing myself on a scale, I began to weigh the signs.

Sometimes, You Know, But It's Hard to Let Go

Time moved on, but I stood still.
I never saw it coming.
I recall the signs.
I heard the voice—a soft, melodic drumming.
I felt a feeling in my gut, but I tried to ignore it.
It felt like something really bad, so I chose not to explore it.
My ears would ring; my palms would sweat—at times, my eye would twitch.
It told me something wasn't right, but I quickly silenced that bitch.

Instead, I smoked my cigarettes.
I fogged my thoughts and mind.

60

I walked around with foggy eyes and kept my feelings
confined.

I never told him what I felt because he'd lie and get me
mad.
I didn't' want him to know that I knew he was being
bad.
I blamed it on my circumstance;
"I'm just too far away.
I hate this school. I'm going home, and home is where
I'll stay."

I sabotaged my concentration and put a hold on my
education.
I wanted him to stay with me and dead the silly
sensations.

Yes, it really felt silly to me,
But I kept getting the notion
That he was being unfaithful to me.
I thought our hearts were filled with devotion.

His mother tried to warn me to find a friend on the
side.
I thought, "How rude to ask me to betray your son!
Haven't you an ounce of pride?"

Although the signs would come and go, I vowed I'd
always love him.
But I never vowed to love myself;

61

My thoughts were always of him.

Each time another message came, I chose to yell at
God.
I couldn't understand why God would make loving him
so hard.

He cheated on me while I was away.
He had another lover.
A baby was conceived, and within nine months,
That lover became a mother.

It broke my heart to think that he could ever love
another.
It broke my heart because my seed was first, but I was
not his first child's mother.

I found out by happenstance;
I wasn't supposed to know.
But someone told me to my face—
I couldn't help but let it show.
I cried for days;
I felt depressed.
I thought my life would end.
I thought, "How could he do this to me? I thought he
was my friend."

For years he would apologize, and I could tell that it
was all lies.
Instead of feeling hatred for him, I still felt butterflies.

After a while, I was sick and tired of being sick and tired. It seemed as if he was intentionally coming back, just to reject me and abandon me. I was tired of letting him back in. It would be great when we were together, but I'd feel the pain of being alone and unloved again the moment he left. I felt betrayed and rejected. The love was covered in pain, but the pain got covered by *anger*!

Lemme Come Too

I was still masturbating when I realized what was going on.
Masturbation of the mind can take place when you're all alone,
Contemplating what to do and facing the unknown.

I stopped for a moment—took a mental time out
To ponder this thing and try to figure it out.

The revelation toyed with me,
Then my nerves got plucked
'cause I finally figured it out—

My Mind Had Been Fucked!

I was seriously intrigued by the thought of it all,
So I let go a little so the walls would begin to fall.

Everyone loves a good one—don't you agree?

63

I just want to be consenting and know you're fucking me.

So, don't toy with my emotions because you think I'm not smart.
At least give the privilege of getting a condom for my heart.

These stupid-ass games are nothing but a

Mental Screw,

So stop fucking my mind

'cause I wanna come too!

The anger grew inside me day by day. I felt so disempowered. I walked around in a fog and closed my heart and mind to any possibility of ever finding *true* love. My thoughts, actions and behaviors weren't working. I began to go to church with hopes that somehow God would ease my pain. It worked for a while too!

I finally began to believe that I really mattered. I studied my Bible diligently. I sat at the feet of wise elders. I connected with powerful women in the church. I felt the love of God. Years continued to fly by. I began to set new goals, enrolled back in school, and felt myself breathing again. I had just ended an on-again, off-again relationship with Him #3.

That's when Him #2 came back.

Hoodwinked

Closed heart, closed mind,
In search of love divine,
Searching for myself, but in need of assistance,
On the right track with much persistence.

Working on self was a really tough job,
But I stayed strong and persevered, and it really wasn't
that hard.

In the midst of my journey,
I heard a knock at love's door.
I panicked at first, and then fell to the floor.
While on the floor, I sought God, and I prayed.
The key was still turning—on the floor, I stayed.

I was scared as hell and didn't know what to do.
Then, the key opened my heart, and I was pleased to
see you.
As I set the table and let you in,
You stroked the woman in me, and I felt warm within.

I held a fortress up over my heart
But surrendered as you carefully tore it apart.
While I tried to hold on to the last remains,
You caressed my heart with affirmation to help me
release the pain.

You stroked me with words and hugged my emotions.
66

You said it was all about me, and I felt the devotion.
My self-esteem grew day by day
From working on myself and those wonderful things
you'd say.
While working on me, I slipped and stumbled at times,
But you helped me back up and said, "Everything
would be fine."

You assured me there was nothing to worry about,
And while I stayed on the path, you detoured and took
another route.

Honesty, integrity, unconditional love—I've been
seeking these things from the Man above.
I prayed to Him daily—about me—about you.
I even thanked Him and praised Him for reuniting us
two.

You stroked my insecurities whenever I cried,
Then invalidated everything with an unnecessary lie.
I was your girlfriend before, and then, I became your
friend.
Who knew that by becoming your woman, it would all
come to an end.

Had I known back then what I now know,
I would have continued to conceal my feelings and
never let them show.
I would have remained your friend
So I could respect you still.

67

*If we got together at any time, it would be of my free
will.*

In the past, I was different;
I knew where I stood.
*Our secret rendezvous were special, and the loving
was real good.*
*I made a conscious choice back then—to be with it or
not.*
*But you tried to take my choice away with your greedy,
selfish plot.*

I tried to love and trust you.
*I tried to understand why you couldn't explain why
you do what you do.*
*I tried not to think that you consciously wanted to
ruin me.*
*I tried to understand the man that declared he wanted
to marry me.*
*I wanted to believe you. I wanted to believe that you
cared.*
But love without truth and trust will not go anywhere.

I planned for the future and invested in you.
*I included you in my dreams and everything I set out
to do.*
I became my pro self just to make you feel good,
*'cause I thought that as your woman, it was OK, and I
could.*

So, one little lie turned into big big this,
And I'm so disappointed because what I thought we
had, I will miss.

I once gave you the lead, "Take my hand, Boo. I'll
follow."
If you loved me for real, your pride you will swallow.

I'm now placing God first in all that I do,
And as I pray for answers, I hear it's time to release
you.
I remember once praying that God prepare me for you.
Now, my prayer is that He does some work on you too.

I'm ready to focus and get back to me,
As I learn to forgive you, my heart will be open and
free.

All these things are on my mind when I think,
And the recurring conclusion is that I've been
Hoodwinked!

Rewriting the Script

I've learned much about myself and how *I* show up in relationships with boys and men. As I continue to educate myself about myself, I accept that there is still more to learn. I'm still on my learning line from my experience with Him #3.

My experience with Him #3 was a combination of my experiences with Him #1 and Him #2. Him #3 was the most impactful teacher of all. By the time I met him, I was finally an adult. However, I still didn't know my worth or how to articulate or envision what I wanted. My self-esteem was depleted.

Him #2 still called or popped up from time to time, but in an effort to release him for *good*, Him #3 seemed like the perfect solution.

In my experience with Him #3, I began to see things differently. My desire for sex and my perception of love didn't feel the same. Sex with Him #3 wasn't fun and adventurous. Him #3 was a cheater, but because my esteem was so low, I tolerated it and dismissed my intuition because I didn't want to be alone.

I surrounded myself with children. My house was the *kiddie hangout* and when I wasn't surrounded by *"the kids,"* I hung out with my friends.

I found comfort in the love and validation I received from my lifelong friends. They became my sisters and brothers. I experienced genuine, loving, authentic connections with each of my friends. It was important for me to know that everybody wasn't interested in hurting me. We had a blast! We celebrated on birthdays, holidays and get-togethers. I hosted annual New Year's Eve celebrations at my home. I masked the feelings of abandonment and rejection that I was feeling. I smiled, made jokes and enjoyed the company of my brothers and sisters, but once I had an opportunity, I would escape to my bedroom or the lock myself in the bathroom to cry like a baby. I often wondered how it was possible to feel loved and unloved at the same time.

I embraced a new love for food. I ate when I felt emotional. I ate when I was happy, sad, angry, or confused. I settled for less than what I wanted because I didn't believe I was worthy of love from *Him*.

The *Hims* in my life served a divine purpose. The themes of each relationship were the same. I was the leading lady in the script of my life, and the leading male changed each time I received an Oscar for Best Supporting Actress. I positioned myself in the role of director, and I was ready to rewrite the script.

I began to read self-help books and attend personal development workshops and motivational lectures. I was committed to healing. I enrolled at Inner Visions Institute for Spiritual Development, and my life changed forever.

I finally saw what I was doing. I accepted ownership, responsibility, and accountability for my actions in each relationship. The four fingers pointing back to me as I pointed the finger were all the information I needed to accept that I am the common denominator in my life experiences.

I sought balance. I chose to honor my healing process as I did my *work*. I didn't want to taint my efforts by doing the same thing differently in love relationships. I learned that forgiveness is a state of mind and not a thing to do. My desire was to live in conscious forgiveness so I could drop back into the love and release the padlock from my heart. I chose not to be in another relationship until I learned to love myself. However, I still experienced *flesh hunger*. In the midst of my healing journey, opportunity knocked, and I answered.

Doogie OWser

It all started with a simple request—
My computer conked out, and I began to feel stressed.
It was down for a week—the hardware had crashed.
I was pissed the hell off, ready to throw it in the trash.

The buttons I pushed wouldn't even turn on.
As I yearned for it to be fixed, I remained a woman
scorned.
Finally, I decided to call a technician.
I knew he could fix it like a revved-up ignition.

His diagnosis proved to be true.
The power surge had blown, and he knew just what to
do,
He took my tower and operated at his home.
He came back to my house, and with some
contemplation,
Began his little scheme of pure manipulation.

The kids had gone out, and we were all alone.
He told me I was lucky that I called and found him
home.
I thanked him again and smiled at the thought
That he was checking me out. It was his eyes that I
caught.

Scanning my large titties and lickin' his lips,

Staring at my nipples as they poked out a bit.
As he ran his corny game, my intentions were the
same
...'cause I was feelin' quite sexy, and my juices I could
not tame.

I sat quietly and took a breath 'cause this reality
Reminded me of my womanhood and sensuality.
For quite some time, my body felt shut down and gone,
But the little computer geek was
turnin' my ass on!

He took off his glasses and looked straight at me.
He told me he was thinking of cosmetic surgery.
Now, being myself, I couldn't help it at all;
I joked and asked him, "What... you're replacing your
balls?"

With a nerdy snicker and intellectual pride,
He said, "Actually, I was thinking of increasing my
size.
I used to be 9 inches, and now, I'm 10, but I'm going for
13."
Then, I watched him grin.

My eyebrow raised, and I began to interrupt
Because this nerdy muthafucka was giving me a
mental fuck.
He jumped up before I could utter a word.
He said, "It's better if I show you;
74

Hey, I know it's absurd.
I have pictures if this all is too graphic for you."
As my juices were boiling, I said, "Yes, pictures. All
right."
But when I looked at the pictures, I knew I was getting
laid lovely that night.

My face did not lie as I stood there in shock.
My little nerdy friend then pulled out his cock.
As sweat fell from my brow right onto his dick,
He invited me to take a lick.
Boy, was I tempted—it was big as hell!
But I stopped myself and said, "Robin, whachoo doin'?
What the hell!"

All of a sudden, it was animal attraction,
As I stood up attempting to avoid the distraction.
I wanted the geek;
I didn't give a fuck.
He spoke my thoughts and asked,
"So, is a brother in luck?"

My alter ego came out and about
I told his ass, I'd make him scream and shout.
He told me he could go for three hours each time.
I said, "Stop talkin' shit and wastin' my time."

I was feelin' mighty sexy as he sucked hard on my
breasts.

75

I quickly laid all fat insecurities to a ceasing, halting
rest.
He tried to take off my pants, but I had to stand up.
For a second, I was embarrassed—then, I said, "Aw,
what the fuck!"

I pulled them down while standing up.
He thrust me on the couch.
He said, "Girl, I'm gonna tear that pussy up."
I sarcastically responded, "Oh, yeah—um hm—ouch."

"Oh, yeah! You think I'm jokin'!" is all I heard him
speak
'cause he threw my legs up in the air and crawled
between my knees.
He threw his head between my legs and came up to see
what I'd say,
But I was like, "Aw, yeah, aw, yeah—today's my lucky
day!"

I shoved his head right back in place and let him go for
the kill
'cause I was thoroughly enjoying his impromptu
eating skills.
I felt my body come back to life.

I panted and screamed and panted some more.
After about fifteen minutes, he was still on the floor.
He rose for air with a nerdy little grin,
Lookin' just like Steve Urkel—divin' in again.

76

I said to myself, "Well, goddamn! That's enough."
I lifted his head and let out a slight "huff."

Irresponsible and nasty—I know, I know,
But I wanted to feel his manhood come out my big toe.
Animal attraction, pure satisfaction,
Feelin' good in my body—then we both started
laughin'.

Ok—so perhaps I mighta, coulda, woulda, should,
But I didn't, and I forgive myself.
Hey, that shit was good.
It was good to feel good from head to toe.
It was good to let go and go with the flow.
My body is happy and so am I.
I release all judgments and asking myself why.

Perhaps as I learn to love the me that I see,
I will learn to stop judging, be free, and just be.

I forgive myself for right now and before.
I forgive myself for judging myself as some sort of
whore.
I forgive myself for having that animal attraction
with Doogie OWser on that spontaneous night
without even using protection.
I forgive myself for feeling bad
About that irresponsible act that me feel glad.
I forgive myself for hating my body and judging myself
as a sucker.

I accept that big or small—I'm still
a sexy motherfucka!

And So It Is

Into Spirit

Awakening

I was committed to taking the necessary steps to look at and identify the motivations behind my intentions. Clearly, my ways of being were unacceptable. I was clear about the impact of *learned behavior*, and I was ready to accept ownership and responsibility for what my daughter and niece would learn from me.

My spirit was calling for awakening, but I had no reference of what was happening in and through me.

I joined St. Paul Community Baptist Church where I first experienced a conscious connection to the presence of God and learned the principles of Sankofa, a West African concept of the Adinkra tribe, which means it's not wrong to go back for that which you have lost, relinquished, or forgotten.

My soul continued to seek truth. I was content at St. Paul, but still felt an absence of fulfillment and joy. I diligently read the Bible, randomly opening pages and highlighting a new scripture each day. I felt connected to God. I had questions. I wanted answers. I felt that God spoke to me every Sunday morning. Although the sanctuary was always packed, in my heart and mind, there was no one else in the room, but God and I.

I felt as if God was requesting something from me. In hindsight, I was clear about what God was asking me to do, but I felt unworthy of such a calling. I acted as if I didn't hear or know *when I really did.*

I recall Reverend Youngblood's charge to the congregation to "follow the coattail of someone already doing what you want to do." That's when I began to *own it.*

God was guiding me to accept my calling as a vessel of love, support, and healing. I sought my mentor of choice.

I finally met up with her at George Fraser's Power Networking Conference in 2004. I now know the power of intention, and I can now declare that I manifested my desire to meet a master who was already doing what I felt I was called to do.

I knew that Iyanla Vanzant wrote books and facilitated workshops that empowered people. I knew that she was a motivational speaker, and after reading and identifying with her story, I wanted to learn from her. Her books gave me a sense of hope, and I often dreamed of the day I would write my first book and be able to be a vessel of hope for someone else.

On the night Iyanla spoke, I was confident that I'd connect with her. I sought to meet her with all her books in hand. I would get an autograph if nothing more. I waited patiently in line to speak to her, but she wasn't signing books. I guess the look of defeat on my face might have prompted what came next. She suggested I wait on the side until everyone left. I did, and she signed my books.

I seized the opportunity to tell her that I wanted to learn from her and that her books had changed my life. She told me about the Wonder Woman Weekend, a weekend intensive she facilitated with a team of coaches and healers. She gave me her business card, mentioned her institute, and suggested I go on the website for more information.

I attended the Wonder Woman Weekend in 2005. My experience at the Wonder Woman Weekend workshop was the divine precursor to my transformed life. I later learned that the "institute" would support me in manifesting what I said I wanted. I declared that by the completion of the three-year program, I would become a Spiritual Life Coach and finally "help" people so *their* lives wouldn't be so *messed up*. I created a laundry list of people I knew would benefit from having me as their coach. I had no idea that my life would begin to unravel, and I would discover so many unidentified, untouched, and unappreciated aspects of myself.

God Spoke to Me

Butt-ass naked—dark, candle-filled room,
Just sitting in the bathtub, rubbing my womb.
It was a Saturday night—that night, I stood still.
I was talking to myself, but I began to feel chills.
Suddenly, it hit me—it was my higher self I was
talking to.
I spoke to God as His presence filled the room.
It was a comforting feeling ya know.
I just knew.

I questioned why and what have I done to myself.
God touched me and hugged me and said,
"I'm here to help."
I cried, and I prayed, and I prayed, and I cried.
And as God comforted me, the heaviness began to
subside.

I asked if my actions were pleasing to Him.
I asked because I wanted to know how to begin again.
I asked Him to block barriers hindering my success.
As I became vulnerable, I really confessed.

I cried some more and told God I felt broken.
I was authentic and honest;
I mean downright outspoken!
I asked Him to heal my heart to love myself
unconditionally.

84

As the sweat poured from my face, and the tears rolled
from my eyes,
God in His greatness, rocked with me.

I asked that he heal my wounds and help me know who
I am.
I confessed that I had become a human doormat for an
undeserving man.
I couldn't reciprocate love to any other because I felt
afflicted.
I felt so hurt and was full of guilt.
I felt so conflicted.
My hardened heart didn't allow me to love.
I needed guidance from the Man above.

I cried some more as I stifled the words to say.
Then asked God to guide me through and take the pain
and guilt away.
Something inside me wouldn't let the past go.
I held on so long—on the outside, it showed.

I piled on extra pounds and stopped caring about my
body.
I didn't know how to forgive and sat at home,
having pity parties.
I prayed some more because I knew God was there.
I prayed that He remove the feelings of agony and
despair.
When I was done praying, I prayed for the souls

*Who helped me to get where I was and encouraged me
to set goals.*

*I kept a journal of my progress and fell asleep
reviewing it.
I awoke to my alarm set to 98.7 Kiss.
The preacher for the day was answering my prayer.
As early as it was, I heard him loud and clear.
The night before, I asked God to show me the purpose
for my life.
As the preacher kept preaching, I sat there and cried.*

*"God wants you to kick down doors and barriers to get
to where He needs you to be because there are people
waiting behind those doors and barriers who don't
know how to get out, who need you to get them out.
Heal yourself so you can heal others."*

*That was God's message, and in a matter of time,
Fireworks and sirens began to clutter my mind.
Shut up, I thought. I can't hear the preacher!
But God's soft melodic whisper said,
"Robin, did I reach ya?"
I was baffled, confused... not focused at all,
But God spoke louder and said,
"Robin, answer my call."*

*I cried in gratitude from the events of the night.
Throughout my body, I felt God holding me tight.
His comforting presence made me feel loved.*

86

I wanted to embrace Him. I wanted to trust.

*I got a phone call that morning from my spiritual
sista.*
I said hello. She said, "Hey, it's Melissa."
We shared, and I talked about the events of my night.
*I told her I felt God's presence and to trust Him just
feels right.*

I needed to go to church to praise God for His word.
I needed Him to know that I listened, and I heard.
I waited for a word about faith from Hebrews 11.
*But was shocked to hear the scripture. It was Psalms
27.*

The Word was on fear, and right from the start,
*The preacher taught about the condition of a hardened
heart.*
Another prayer answered; God spoke to me again!
He was telling me that my healing had to begin within.

I had to go through in order to come out.
It was an aha moment, and I wanted to shout.

I now pray daily and seek God's assistance.
I am specific in prayer, and I remain persistent.
God's plan for my life is becoming clear.
*Especially since I began to listen and know when He is
near.*
I now look for God in everything I do.

87

My daily prayer is that my mind be renewed.
I know God loves me, and I know that He cares.
I took TheRiteStep into my life and increased my
prayers.

I am becoming a scripture for people to read.
With the Lord's guidance, I can help them succeed.
God is my salvation—my rock.
His love and guidance are helping me to
Step Outta da Box!

Acknowledging the God Within

As my consciousness lifts, my vibration shifts.
I ain't got no time for that triflin' shit.
It's time to move on... advance to higher levels,
'cause I'm elevating in God consciousness and
stomping out the devil.
I thank You, God, for putting rhythm to my rhyme.
I thank You most of all 'cause You are always right on
time.
As soon as I start to wallow or hammer another nail,
You send someone to remind me of my purpose on this
trail.
The journey I'm on right now is nowhere near
complete.
The steps I take are a constant reminder of what I'm
charged to teach.
As You make me wise and teach me—You show me
how to Be.
No longer will Human Doing fit the likes of me.
I'm striving, Lord, to feel You... I know You are within.
I know in order to heal myself, within I must begin.

I know that when I look into the reality of my world,
What I will see is a reflection of a once frightened little
girl.
My inner child is growing, not in age, but in mind.
The child in me dances gleefully each time the cord
unwinds.

89

I'm clear that I have lassoed an invisible cord around my heart.
I'm clear that I have closed it so it wouldn't be torn apart.
Now that I'm conscious of what I've done,
I'm ready to reverse it.
If I don't feel You now,
I know I will as I continue to rehearse it.
Fake it till you make it—that's what most people say.
I know I'll make it very soon because You've already lit the way.
I love You, God. I love this path.
I love all people on it.
I love each lesson I learn as I stumble right up on it.
I know now that You've been waiting for me to turn to You;
That time has come, and I'm ready, Lord.
I know You'll bring me through,
As I partake of this healing journey and elevate to You.
Allow me, Lord, the discernment of acknowledging what to do.
I thank You in advance for making me aware.
I thank You for acknowledging my tantrum, screams, cries, and my prayers.
You're not only up there; You also live in me.
And that's the part I work so hard in striving to believe.
I never knew to feel and see the Light that shines within me.

I've always thought that Heaven was a place where
people in white robes would be.
I've found the Light. I've searched within, and now, I
know You more.
I now know that Heaven is a state of mind;
There is no gated door.
I used to think that one more curse or one more
negative thing
Would close the door forever, and I'd never meet the
King.
Now that I have faith and tools,
I know just what to do
I'll breathe and pray and meditate
And call and shout to You.
I know You always hear me.
I know each time You speak.
I know the days you make me strong when I tell myself
I'm weak.
I can write forever about who You are in me.
You are my Light and my Love—my Creativity.
My sacrifice to You, my God, was cutting off my Locs.
Please show me how to change my thoughts to get out
of this Box!

Praise Held Hostage

My praise was held hostage in a jail called my mind.
I searched everyone else's meaning of this praise I tried
to find.

My praise was hostage.
I simply did not know God.
I didn't know how to release and let go,
So praise I could not find.

I never felt the God inside.
I never felt His presence.
I never knew how great I was,
So how could I embrace His essence?

My praise was held hostage,
Locked somewhere in my chest.
The praise in me searched desperately to awaken from
its rest.

One day, I fell down on my knees.
I asked for God's direction.
To my surprise, the God within surfaced with
affection.

I began to see that God lives in me.
God illuminated my heart.
The pieces began to coincide within;
No longer were they apart.

The God I thought was way up there and would punish
me when I'm bad
Revealed to me so easily, the blessings that I have.
I counted my blessings one by one;
I thanked God for my life.
The self-inflicted scars I caused began to heal
When I released the knife.

My praise was held hostage.
God showed me how to be.
He gave me vision. She nurtured me
With sensitivity.

Generational traits from long ago began to surface in
my head.
I thought about Sankofa and looked back to move
ahead.

My praise was held hostage
Until I began to nurture my soul.
I sought support, and God provided, so at Inner
Visions I enrolled.

My praise was held hostage.
I gave life to drama and victimhood,
Because I always got defensive and felt misunderstood.

My praise was held hostage,
Because I was unwilling to surrender.
I gave life to the negative ego,
And I had not learned to be tender.

I learned to breathe consciously. I learned to pray and
meditate.
I learned to trust that inner voice and muster up some
faith.
Finally, the inner voice proclaimed,
"I know you can get through this."
Just call on God and feel Him, dear;
There's really nothing to it.

So I chose to speak of all that I was thankful for.
I chose to thank Him for the times He nurtured all my
sores.
I thanked God for pulling me through those times
when I felt stuck.
I thanked God for shining light when I ran stories
amuck.

I give thanks and praise to God for mercy and for grace.
I give thanks and praise to God for purpose.
I give thanks to God for praise.

I thanked God for all the times She held me in Her bosom.
I worshipped God for saying I can when I believed I couldn't.
I thanked God for the lessons I learned thus far.
I praise Him for enlightening me with lessons from my car.

I thank you, God, for showing up.
When it gets empty, you fill my cup.
I praise you, God, because You are the Truth.
You not only show me who to Be;
You tell me what to do.

I praise you, God, 'cause you're right on time.
You add the rhythm to my rhyme.

You guide me in the right direction,
And yes, God, I feel your love and affection.
I find slumber in you when I need protection.

Wait—I just got high from that spiritual injection!

Don't stop me now—no need for correction.
I'm basking in divine connection.

95

So I breathe in Life,
And I breathe in Love,
And if you're on your path, too,
You know exactly what I'm speaking of.

God's Everlasting Love

God's Everlasting Love,
That of an ancestor whose soul speaks through her
grandchild.

God's Everlasting Love,
That of the first love that broke your heart twenty
times over and over again,
That feeling that kept you yearning for more—

Never giving up.
Going back this one last time for more—The muscle it
took to finally declare
Enough.

God's Everlasting Love,
The look on a mother's face when her child asks for
reassurance,
The stern face and poised body that spits out that
weak response...
Not sure if it's right, but trusting the answers will
come.

God's Everlasting Love,
The blessed goodness that comes from the repenting of
sins.

97

God's Everlasting Love
That everlasting love of a man—
Full of Life and Christ consciousness—
Dying on a cross
To save my Soul.

My Soul Speaks

My soul speaks loudest when my faith is put to the
test.
My soul shouts when my body feels weary and
stressed.
My soul speaks loudest when my daughter cries.
Yearning for her daddy and asking me why—
Why we're not together;
Why we can't get along.
Why she feels like it's all her fault as if she did
something wrong.
My souls screams and then speaks aloud
When she does well in school and makes both of us
proud.
My soul will yell and then begin to whisper
When I tuck my child in and lean down to kiss her.
My soul begins to sing when I think of my God,
How He carries me through situations that to bear
seems too hard.
My soul speaks for my niece yearning for her parents.
Then, my soul tells me I'm not her mom or her dad,
But I can be the parent she wishes she had.
My soul speaks the loudest when I write what I'm
feeling,
When I realize my strengths and focus on my healing.
My soul is like a speaker for all to hear.
My soul is the voice in my inner ear.

Still Under Construction
(Inspired from "Kids Under Construction" by
Marva Collins)

I'm still under construction
Building character and poise each day.

I'm still under construction;
God's shaping and molding me in every way.

I'm still under construction.
Don't judge this book by its cover.
I'm on the road to success with many new things to
discover.

I'm still under construction.
Maybe the thought never crossed your mind.
Think back to your youth;
Have you ever felt confined?
"Because I said so. Sit down! Shut up! Come here! Stop
that! I'ma beat your butt!"

I try to behave and remember what I've learned,
But sometimes to understand, I have to get burned.
I'm a sponge for information.
I'm studying God's ways.
I want to lead by positive example and do just what I
say.

I'm still under construction,
100

But I'm moving on with the light of God.
He's guiding me every step of the way,
And I'm comforted by His staff and His rod.
I fall down at times, but I will always rise,
Because I'm growing in the power of the resurrected
Christ.

I'm still under construction,
And God's not finished with me yet.
Please be patient as I learn to be me,

'Cause this Kid is still under construction;
The paint is still wet!

Comfort in the Clouds

In the midst of the clouds, there is fog and gray.
There is a lingering stillness that I want to obey.

In the midst of the clouds, there is patience and ease.
It's the highway to heaven,
Calling out to me.

In the midst of the clouds, I feel love and protection.
Although I cannot see, I am clear on my direction.

There is acceptance and joy in the midst of the clouds.
My soul cries out,
And God smiles 'cause He's proud.

Today I basked in the calm before the storm.
I basked in the peace as I watched the rain form.
I took a deep breath;
I took it all in,
Then stood there mesmerized as I heard the rain
begin.

As it poured down raining, it all seemed so clear.
While in the midst of the clouds,
I am being prepared.
I know something's coming;
I'm not sure how strong.
I know that the calmness doesn't always last for long.

I can grab an umbrella, seek shelter, or hide.
I can find external refuge before going inside.
I can fear getting wet or ruining my hair,
Or I can embrace the blessings of my lessons
And release all my fears.

It's a time to get still and bask in the glory.
It's the faith in knowing there's a joyful end to the
story.

I could not see as the storm took flight,
But I maintained clear vision through my internal
light.
I was so amazed.
I felt at ease.
I prayed for more blessings
In lessons such as these.

God guided me through;
I was warned in advance.
I suddenly found myself
In a hypnotic trance.

As the clouds danced,
My faith enhanced.
I took another deep breath
And strengthened my stance.

Before I was ready,
The rain poured down.
There was no more time
To be messin' around.
Blindly, I walked
In the midst of the clouds.
I focused on God
As my spirit allowed.
I welcomed the gray
And the fog from the storm.
I blessed the sky
As I watched it transform.
I searched for the lesson;
My vision was clear.
Suddenly, the storm
Began to disappear.
As I watched it subside
And begin to go.
I remembered the Law—
As above, so below.

So, when it rains,
Pours, and thunders loud,
I think back to the calmness
In the midst of the clouds.

104

Basking in the Silence

In the silence, there is depth.
There is long, lingering forgiveness and love.
There is breath.

In the silence, the waves of the ocean roar.
In the silence, I am free to explore.
The silence allows me to soar through my thoughts.
I dismiss what needs to be released and explore what
needs to be sought.

As I sit in silence, I shift my perception.
I focus on the Most High and seek His protection.
I snuggle in Her bosom for comfort and cover.
Then, lay myself down and rest in the Great Mother.

I surrender in silence.
I am calm and still.
In the silence, the possibilities of my dreams become
real.
In the silence, I cry, and I know it's OK
To release the drama without having anything to say

In the silence, I die to the old and rebirth the new.
In the silence, I hear the voice of God and know just
what to do.
This silent time is full of love and compassion.
My desires are of God.
I expect what I imagine.

I co-create with Spirit.
I ask the ancestors for guidance.
I comfort my inner children and release the defiance.

In the silence, I am Healed.
I am whole and complete.
I validate myself, and it feels oh so sweet.
In the silence, I am showered in unconditional love.
I am free to soar and explore like a white dove above.

I am free to breathe and enjoy the flow
Like the ripples in the ocean and the dolphins below.
I am beautiful and light like the fresh fallen snow.

In the silence, I am free!
I am healed!
I am powerful beyond measure.
In the silence, I find ecstasy, intimacy, and pleasure.

Thank you, God, for the beauty of this time.
Thank you, God, for the rhythm in my rhyme.
As I move forward through my trials and tests,
I'll remember this moment and remain at rest.

For this and so much more, I am grateful and relaxed.

Ase'

Thanks and Praise to the Most High for This Journey

I thank you, God, for my extended family.
Thank you for showing me and teaching me a new way
to be.
During the times I feel weary and weak,
I can call on my family any day of the week.
It's so wonderful to know that I'm aligned with God.
It cancels the belief that life has to be hard.
My awareness has elevated, my energy shifted;
My spirits are high, and my expectancy lifted.
Creativity flows through me to show that I'm gifted.
The anointing falls on me as negativity is sifted.

I thank you, God, for the mirrors of me.
Thank you for showing me and teaching me a new way
to be.

When I sat in lack, drama, and self-destruction,
I began to experience a spiritual abduction.
My mind, soul, and body were under construction.
My negative ego underwent massive obstruction.

I heard God's call and finally replied.
My ego flipped out and fought to survive.
I'm grateful for my ego; it wanted to live.
But with skills, tools and principles, my Spirit now
forgives.

I forgive myself for sitting in lack.
I forgive myself for brutal self-attack.
I forgive myself for feeling unworthy.
I forgive myself for behaving unearthly.
I forgive myself for living a lie.
I forgive myself for limiting my supply.
I forgive myself for denying my worth.
I forgive myself for the untruths I birthed.
I forgive myself for not seeking my mission.
I forgive myself for dishonoring myself and not moving toward my vision.

I love myself for the steps I've made.
I love myself for releasing the masquerade.
I love myself for the work I've done.
Watch out now, world;
My journey's just begun.

Into Me See

Doing the Work

I enrolled at Inner Visions because I had visions of writing books, facilitating empowerment workshops, and empowering people through motivational speeches and lectures. My ultimate dream was to support young girls and women in loving themselves, moving beyond adverse circumstances, and manifesting their dreams... *everything I wanted for myself.* I hadn't acknowledged at the time that all the ideas were divine imprints of my life experiences and my soul's mission.

I walked around in self-righteous, judgmental arrogance, seeing people as broken, "knowing" the Truth for others and focusing my time, energy, and attention on trying to "fix" the world, without a hunch that the world was my reflection, revealing back to me what I looked like, how I behaved, what I felt, and where the healing would begin.

In my second year of study at the Inner Visions Institute for Spiritual Development, we were given an assignment to heal a relationship with someone in our life. Everyone in the class was assigned this project, yet I was the only one in the history of the school who was asked to change the subject of my relationship project from an ex-boyfriend to *myself.*

110

This project brought new awareness and created shifts in certain beliefs I had about myself.

During my three-year rite of passage, I came present to how much I masked. I knew that I masked some things, but I didn't realize the level of untruth that I stood in until completing that project. I never realized how much I avoided myself. I never understood the level of self-loathing, how much fight I had within me, where it came from, or why it lay dormant in my body.

I chose to release my victim story and rewrite the script of my life. I named my project, *"Loving the Me I See."* The inner work felt mundane at first, but in the end, proved just what I needed. My work consisted of an integrated blend of prayer, meditation, conscious breathing techniques, coaching, strategic action steps, cognitive behavioral therapies, energy healing, and mirror meditations.

My inner work is the catalyst for the creation of this book as well as a seven-step healing module I created called E.D.U.C.A.T.E.™ When Spirit really wants me to *get it,* I am supported in reenergizing words through acronyms.

Throughout my introspective process, I learned to E.D.U.C.A.T.E.™ myself about myself and check in with myself.

I learned that healing happens on a cellular level and that my inner work is a consistent process. I was taught that self-mastery is a process and that true mastery comes when I teach what I need to learn, while embracing all that is and seeing each living thing on the planet as a reflection of myself. I integrated and adapted the teachings of all my teachers. Spirit then guided me to create a seven-step healing module so I could apply it to my life and teach it to others.

Examination: *Looking Back in Order to Move Ahead*

Desire: *In Order to Live, Be Willing to D.I.E. (Desire, Imagine, Expect)*

Understanding: *In Order to Understand, Learn to Inner-Stand*

Communication: *Heartfelt Communication Begins Within*

Ask/Advocate: *Request Support and Advocate for Your Worth*

Teach: *Be the Example You Want To See*

Empower: *To Know Myself Is to Consistently E.D.U.C.A.T.E.™ Myself about Myself*

Phase One
I Am...

Growing in the power of the resurrected Christ,
One who falls down time after time, but still... I rise.

I am mother, aunt, daughter, niece, sister, cousin,
friend, confidante.
I am loved by many—resented by some.

I am hated by resentful lovers and people who love to
be resentful.
I am loved by some who resent me but hate to admit it.

I am truthful, blunt, and straightforward.

I am positively motivated and sometimes negatively
influenced.

I am repetitious of some old ways but starting to make
changes....

I am seeking, observing, listening, and awakening.

I am learning day by day.

I am resistant to ask for help, but ready to seek
guidance.

I am fearful of the unknown.

113

I am writer, poet, student, supervisor, subordinate.

I am learning to trust God.

I am in search of self and inner peace.

I am a walking story....

I am living—not chapter by chapter, but sentence by sentence, eagerly turning page by page.

I am in search of the plot for my life.

Phase Two
I Am Fire....

I am the heat that sparks the flame.
Don't come too close or rub me the wrong way,
'Cause if you play with fire,
You will be burned!

In the heat of passion, my flames are Ablaze.
I'll keep you warm with my touch,
Make your manhood rise, and leave you sitting in a
daze.

Talented and gifted,
I can write and recite
All the poetry and rhythmless motion that creeps in
the night.

A true friend to the end,
But be careful not to cross me,
'Cause I might be loyal and caring,
But I'm no Mrs. Softy.

Motivated and centered by God's grace 'cause I'm
blessed,
Sometimes I worry so much I feel stressed.
Inflicted by depression, I was at one time.
Until I realized my worth and added rhythm to my
rhyme,
Recognizing the divinity that lives within me,

115

*I became a Realist Applying Divine Inspiration
through God's Grace Artistically.*

Radigga *is my name, and yes,* I am Fire.
*Color me red or yellow—any color you desire.
At times, the sparks are low, and I have some bad
days,
But on others, I'm* hot
'Cause the fire's ablaze.

*Spark the beast in me, and you're sure to see
The fire getting higher and the Blazin' Bitch that lives
in me.
Stroke the woman in me, and my flames remain calm.
You'll feel my warm spirit, my compassion, my charm.*

I am Radigga*—Half Beast/Half Woman of Desire.*

I am Radigga.
Hell, yes, I am Fire!

Phase Three
I Am ....

I am the Beloved daughter in whom God is well
pleased.
I am learning to love myself,
The me that I see.
I am embracing my potential and loving my face.
I am healing and accepting God's mercy and grace.

I am loving on my body, just as it is now.
I am trusting and faithful; God's showing me how.

I am a writer, and I scribe my truth.
I am a powerful SISTA—healing scars from my youth.

I am loving and gentle, nurturing and kind.
I am releasing the fight that kept me confined.
I am beautiful as I am right now.
I am looking into myself because I made a vow—
To love on myself, to Be who I am,
To validate myself, and be all I can.

I am a powerful SISTA inspired to achieve.
I can do anything I choose to believe.

I am steppin' outta da box of limitation and fear.
I am releasing all doubt until it finally disappears.

I am a work in progress on the road to success.

117

I'm healing right now through the words I confess.
I'm looking back at my life to move forward again.
As I heal from my past, I see deeper within.
I am focused and centered.
I'm steppin' out on faith and into the true me.
I am removing the mask and learning to be.

I am honoring my feelings and releasing the stress.
I am thanking God right now because I know that I'm blessed.

Image and Likeness

I am made in the image and likeness of God on
purpose.
I am an individual expression of God's Love.
Jesus, the Son of God, is the perfect example of Christ
Consciousness.
His life is my guide;
Resurrection is my lifestyle!
I choose to live life to the fullest.
The journey of life is safe.
I am blessed with strengths and talents that assist me
in the harmonious flow of life.
God wants me to succeed.
I am loved, loving, and lovable.
I forgive myself, and I forgive others.
I am abundant and prosperous.

God really wants me to succeed.

I love myself totally and unconditionally.
God says yes to all my prayers.
I am the epitome of Humility, Integrity, and Truth.
I am a servant of God.
I am an expression of Perfect Health.
I am worthy of my own time, energy, and attention.
I am whole.

I hold the pen and punch the keys, yet God is the
writer of the script of my life.
119

Menage Moi

Intimacy
Into Me... see.
I see—into Me.
Into Me... be.
As I envelop and caress my large breasts,
I take a deep breath and release all the stress.

Into Me—Into Me,
Enter Me please.
Enter Me please.
Enter Me with ease....
As I fondle my nipple, I begin to feel a twitch.
It's getting hot down there.
God! Pa—lease... scratch this itch!

It's mind over matter as the pitter starts to patter.

Intimacy
Into Me... see.
See who I am.
Being intimate with Me.
Me?
Yeah... Me!
Feeling free to be with Me.
Feeling free to be as I see into Me.

As I massage my womb, I embrace life and forgive,
Embrace life and forgive in order to live!

I explore my body from head to toe.
Judgment rears its ugly head,
But I breathe and let it go.

Go?
Go!
Release and let go.
Ain't gonna let no judgment interrupt this flow.

Free to feel all of Me,
Free to imagine,
Free to be.
Free to explore inside of Me,
Free to enjoy this intimacy.

Remember Me....

I look in the mirror, and I hear you.
I hear inner voices—screaming, yelling, whining,
crying for attention.
I feel as if I know you, yet... I don't recognize you.
As my eyes well up, I hear a knocking sound—as if
something is trying to get my attention.
Knock, Knock, Knock!
I turn to look behind me, but no one is there.
Knock, Knock, Knock!
What is that? Where is it coming from? Who could it
be?
My eyes leave the mirror, and I begin to remember....
It's coming back to me.

The inner sounds of my soul reveal themselves to me.
I turn to look in the mirror and lift the large, shapeless
skin covering my womb...
Suffocating my vagina!
Guilt! Anger! Pain! Shame!

Then, I remember...
I remember the abortions.
My seeds... the seeds that were conceived when... never
mind....
Stuff it! Turn away! Ignore it!

No... feel it—go there....

Feelings of anger and shame begin to surface.
I am re-membering...
The scrapings! The suctions! The stretching—the
pulling!

I fall to my knees! I want to cry, but the tears will not
fall.
I call out to Him, "God, please forgive me! Help Me,
God!"

I hear the soft melodic voice again, "I already have.
Now, forgive yourself, Beloved."

I forgive myself for judging myself as bad.
I forgive myself for judging myself as a murderer.
I forgive myself for judging myself as careless and
irresponsible.
I forgive myself for judging myself as stupid.
I forgive myself for the choices I made in the past.
I forgive myself for judging the choices I made that
resulted in multiple abortions.
I forgive myself for holding myself captive in a jail of
victimhood.
I forgive myself for searching outside myself for love.
I forgive myself for not trusting God.

Then, I remember... I am committed to my healing and
devoted to loving the Me that I See!

Womb-Did

Because you've done all you could
Because you've served me as you should
Because your intentions were always for good
It's time to be at rest

Because I've used you to please my man
Because you've stretched as far as you can
Because you've withheld all you could stand
It's time to give you rest

You've served your purpose and paid your dues
You held and nurtured my children, despite the abuse
You knew the truth through every excuse
And now I offer you rest

As I rub you down with oils of joy
I whisper affirmations
Each time I reflect on your role in my life
I experience many sensations

You are the divine essence of my womanhood
You are the expression of my femininity
You are the voice of my pain and the melody of my
heart
You are the source of my fertility

From infant to adult
You endured each experience

*Yet you allow me to express myself with joy in sheer
elegance*

*But now it's time to allow you to rest and thank you
for your role
I thank you for enduring it all with me and nurturing
my soul*

*You've taught me that to give birth is a blessing
While guarding and protecting me through each of
life's lessons
I offer an apology for each invalidation
Please accept my love and gratitude. It comes without
hesitation*

*Beloved, you have served me and now can have your
rest
It's time for you to heal, my love – without any more
duress*

*My vow to you is to remember it all. My vow is never
to forget it
Each time I give birth or acknowledge my worth
I'll remember all that my Womb-Did*

Releasin' the Mask Ain't an Easy Task

Learning to love myself was a challenging task,
'Cause for so very long, I wore a mask.
My energy was focused on people and things
That only kept me away from the joy that life brings.
My time was spent delving in other people's affairs,
Instead of spending time with myself and thanking
God I'm still here.

My attention—never centered—always scattered
about.
Now, when it comes to another's matter, I know to
butt out.

As I feel in my body, my spirit is fed.
I spend time with myself and shift the negative
thoughts in my head.
It's not easy going back and looking within,
But the Universe supports me with new spiritual
friends.

I asked God for help. I asked God for direction.
I asked God to show me how to show myself affection.
I asked God to nourish me with wisdom and truth.
The fact I'm still standing is part of that proof.

My prayers have been answered.
My truth is revealed.
I'm learning to uncover those things I concealed.

126

I can finally look in the mirror and release the mask.
What's still hard to believe is that it's all 'cause I
asked.

I've been given a mission; now I'm living it out.
I'm releasing anger, fear, and doubt.
I'm being reconnected, and I'm walking my path.
I'm gonna keep right on steppin';
I ain't turnin' back.

As I walk this path, I am learning to be.
My forgiveness work opens the door to true integrity.
The truth of who I am is a motivating force—
An empowered woman, staying focused on my course.

As I release the mask and learn to be me,
My spirit is lifted; my soul is free.

Phase Four
I Am...

*The Queen in me dances gleefully as I embrace all
aspects of whom I'm charged to be.
Acknowledging my power from head to toe, I identify
stagnant energy and let it go.
I rebuke fear as it attempts to steer.
I instead embrace my vision and hold it very near.
I stare fear in its eyes, and it becomes no big deal,
'Cause I know fear is False Evidence only Appearing
Real.*

**In dedication to Yemoja, Osun and Universal
Goddess energy, I embrace the principles of
Divine Love, Beauty, Nurturing, and
Inner and Outer Harmony.**

I am Balance.

I am Peace.

I am spiritually, mentally, and physically shifted and
lifted.
I am talented, wise, and extremely gifted.
*The many faces of me are so proud to see the
unification of Spirit enveloping me.*

I am caressing my heart with love and forgiveness.

128

I am pouring out libations of sincerity and
compassion to all I know.
I am illuminating my body temple as I nourish myself
with live foods, green foods, nutrients, and undeniable
love.
I am Joy, swinging joyously on the swing of life. There
are ups, and there are downs, yet
I am flying—high—above circumstance, above doubt,
above fear, above projections, because
I am protected by the Light.

I am Light!

*The dark places in my life have been lit, for I now
acknowledge that*
I am the Light I've been looking for.

I am Forgiveness!
I am Green Forgiveness.
I am heart chakra, pulse pumpin', Kelly green
Forgiveness.

*I forgive myself; I forgive my friends; I forgive ex-
lovers; I forgive my family.*

I forgive! I forgive! I forgive!

I am embracing the spirit of forgiveness as I
experience and express the beauty of Unconditional
Love.

I am joy-filled as I breathe in Life and watch my dreams come true.
I am shifting my posture from a slumped down, unsure, insecure hump to a new improved upright, Feminine, Divine, Living Goddess, Made in the Image of My Mother.

I am admiring my face that now illuminates a bright caramel glow that integrates my human self with my higher Goddess self and grounds me with the light of Spirit.

I love me!
I truly love me!

I am releasing....

I release the past. I release rage. I release doubt. I release fear. I release unworthiness, I release I can't. I release emotional upset. I release emotional eating. I release mental, physical, and spiritual clutter. I release obesity and the density of my thinking. I release any and everything standing in the way of my **Divine Beauty.**

I am traveling this journey with Light, Love, Forgiveness, and Expectancy of all that is to come, giving thanks and praise to the Most High Divine Mother Goddess of many names: **Yemoja, Mut, Shakti, Tara, Gaia and more!**

I am grateful for my spiritual guides, ancestors, and angels who are leading me on this journey.
I am elevating in consciousness to the greatness and pleasingly powerful Queen that *I am*.

I am divinely led and passionately inspired to serve by sharing my journey with other SISTAS through my talents and gifts of writing, nurturing, and speaking **my** truth with love, in love, for the sake of **Unconditional Love.**

I am *that* **I am**!
Amen! Ase'! And So It Is!

My Body's Callin'

132

Angerville

My body has been speaking, and I have ignored its call.

What was once a sanctuary, a temple of divine light, has now become a deep, dark, emotion-filled abyss—corrupted with denied feelings, untruths, self-sabotage, and stress-related issues. This temple no longer resembles or personifies the essence of who I really am.

My feet, hard, harboring calluses and corns because I walked down paths with others and forced my feet into shoes that did not fit. I denied myself the comfort and ease of walking my path with trust and faith. Each step I took was a step connecting me to the things I told myself about myself. My feet tried to warn me each time that I dumbed down or stepped into someone else's lane without acknowledging my journey. Sprained ankles, stubbed toes—eventually, I broke my ankle in three places on the left side—the receiving side. Metal plates and pins hold the bone together to remind me. I ignored the warnings and dumbed down to the messages.

My calves are large and muscular. The muscle is still there, though. There's no flab there! None! They just need to be strengthened. Memories of winning relay races, running track, and dancing ballet and jazz begin to surface. I remember... Yes! I remember, as I point my toes... I flex... I point. I see the structure of a well-formed dancer's leg, masked by cellulite and fatty tissue. My face grimaces as I think back to the year that I decided to quit dancing because my "friends" laughed at me and called the art of ballet something that white people and nerds did. I never danced again after that.

These legs were *fast*! I remember winning the relay races against the boys. I was the fastest one! I was determined then... determined to be the best! I trusted then. I believed in myself. I said, "I will win this race," and I did win. I beat the fastest boys on my block. I remember the relay race when I raced the fastest boy in my neighborhood. It was the result of a challenge. He admitted I was fast, but not fast enough to beat him. It was *on!* That inner voice appeared loud and direct again. *"What are you trying to prove?"* I blocked it. I ran. I focused. I needed to catch up. I was winning—then—suddenly... *cluck...* ay- yi- yi- yi. Down I went. It was the first time I sprained my knee—my left knee. The doctor dubbed it a "trick knee" like the football players experience some times. After several "incidents" of my knee getting dislocated again, the doctor showed me how to massage it back into place whenever it was disjointed.

My knees feel weak and achy now... but I remember. I remember when I could sit Indian style and do the butterfly in dance class. Stop playing... not the reggae dance... the *real* butterfly—feet together, knees outward, sitting straight up, and flapping my knees "like a butterfly!" Both feet touched each other, and my knees could touch the floor. The agility and flexibility that once allowed me to move with force and passion now show signs of weakness and fear.

My thighs are heavy. They've carried the weight of the world. These thighs have been ignored, abused, negated, and shunned. I took them for granted. I stopped loving and nurturing them. I allowed them to be pulled, stretched, and laid on by unworthy men who betrayed me, and I now realize that they were the reflection of how I betrayed myself. My thighs are the visual embodiment of the decisions I've made. They harbor the pride that would not allow me to forgive myself for making unhealthy, dishonoring choices. They are the incarnation of the ego that kept me externally focused, avoiding responsibility for my actions and blaming everyone for what *"they did to me."*

Eventually, I was stuck in self-judgment and brutal self-attack.

Between my thighs lay the center of Angerville... a dark lonely place, corrupt with external toxins and debris left over from visitors and strangers who did not care about or honor my sacred temple.

As I unveil the history of Angerville, I realize that these "inconsiderate" souls did not overthrow the queen of the temple; I, the queen, willingly forfeited the title. The more I devalued my temple, the more I dimmed my divine light. Darkness surrounded my vagina and traveled up through my womb, infecting it with yeast infections. Swampy, muddy, external toxins mixed with internal toxins formed a hideous cave—a dirty mess in my stomach.

There were unprotected entries of unworthy intruders. Life was conceived. My womb was stretched and tugged, gnawed at, and twisted from abortions.

My intestines were clogged with toxic foods and repressed emotions—unchewed meat and starches I stuffed in my mouth to avoid the uncomfortable feelings that surfaced each time another baby was conceived or each time another unworthy intruder was given my approval to enter.

Embarrassed by my actions and afraid to admit to anyone else or myself that I was the only one responsible for the demise of my temple, I, the queen finally allowed myself to move beyond the abuse from unworthy intruders. Instead, I found another method to abuse the temple further. I began to eat and smoke to numb the pain. Food comforted me. Smoking fogged my heart and mind.

The temple no longer resembled that of Power and Light. It was no longer the innocent vessel of love, wholeness, and joy. Feeling sorry for myself, but unwilling to be exposed or vulnerable, I masked my emotions, creating disconnect from my heart... disconnect from my temple. No one was allowed in, and no one was allowed out of Angerville.

It was dark and lonely, stifling and cold. My power center was covered by debris. As time moved on, anger, rage, fear, and doubt overthrew the queen. I lost sight of my potential to love and be loved. My heart hid behind a thick, dark fog, and I wondered what life would be like if I could learn to love myself. I wondered what my heart would look like if I redeemed my power and healed myself. Feeling defeated and unaccepted by God, I walked through life, bottled up in Angerville, unwilling to free myself...

Until Today!

My Body Speaks....

Whachoo think I wanna do?
You've been holding me back too long.
I tried to tell you before, but you kept singing that
same ol' song.
I'll lose weight in the summer.
I don't care if I'm fat.
And you know yo ass was lying, acting like a little brat.
Who'd you think you were hurting by gaining all that
extra weight?
It then became a habit to pile food on your plate.
When you were sad, you grabbed some food.
You never seemed to care.
I stretched and begged and cried for help,
But you deemed life unfair.
I've been talking to you all this time,
But you just wouldn't listen.
Even when I reached out to you,
You preferred division.

I was hurt and embodied the pain
When you gave me away.
You felt you owed someone something,
But you always made Me pay.

You pimped me, and you sold me out.
You treated me like dirt.
But I loved you every step of the way.
I knew that you were hurt.

So, now that you acknowledge me,
I'd like to make a deal.
I believe the wounded part of you is finally ready to
heal.
Trust the process—I'm waiting for you.
Just put your mind into it.
Allow Spirit to guide you, Boo.
There's really nothing to it.

You've made the choice to heal the disconnection,
And I truly feel your love and affection.
Although you ate for emotional protection,
You forgot to seek the Lord's direction.
So, now that you know what to do...

Let's do this, girl! I'm counting on you!

A Message from Power

Beloved Robin,

You have held me hostage long enough! Although there are times that you've acknowledged me and allowed yourself to express the power within, the experience of being held captive has been far more impactful on your self-worth and stifles your anointing.

I hear your cries as you search for me, but it was you, dear Robin, who placed me here. I feel as if I'm being punished each time you choose to negate me, keep me confined, or enable me by allowing someone else's power to dominate me.

We are one, yet you have been playing small, allowing others to seem bigger, smarter, happier, and more worthy than you are. I've attempted to break out and show up, but you fought to keep me confined and argued for lack and limitation. It's as if you forgot your unification with me... your unification with God! I am Power. I am the Power of God within you!

I'm trapped in here. I've been speaking to you through your Mind, Body & Spirit, but you have yet to acknowledge me. Now is the time, Robin. It's time for you to experience and express the Power Within. I need you to get me out of here!

140

Look... I'm speaking to you through your body. These mirror meditations are working. Walk closer to the mirror... yup... while you're still naked. Look. I acknowledge your tears. It's all right. It's OK to feel... acknowledgment of what you're feeling is the first step to healing. You're almost there... a little farther down... that's it... past your face, below your neck... right there! Focus... listen to your body. Those breasts... those are nurturing breasts. The size does not matter. It doesn't matter if your breasts are big or small. What matters is that they symbolize the nurturer in you. Embracing the Power Within will support you in your role as a nurturer.

Now... down a little farther... uh huh... you're there. Notice the penitentiary where I've been serving time. Allow those tears to continue to cleanse you of the judgments you've held. Wash away the outdated stories you've told yourself about yourself. You are not your circumstance. Release judgment. Forgive yourself. Accept yourself. Love yourself, and embrace your inner power to get up!

I'm here, Robin. I am inside of you, and you have the power *to experience and express all I am in, through, and as you.*

I'm trapped in your stomach... the power center. I am surrounded by toxic waste. It's dark and gloomy in here, where there should be light. My cellmate is Vulnerability. She and I have plotted this intervention for some time now. Vulnerability has not yet acquired the courage to reveal herself. She still fears the judgments. The warden here is Anger, yet she likes to be called Rage because she's known for sabotaging the path to Forgiveness and Love. She has correction officers all over the place! I'm familiar with some. Shame and Doubt always walk together with their heads down. However, Lack and Fear are the worst! They hold the key to my cell, and whenever they get the urge, they dangle the key in front of Vulnerability and me, daring us to take it.

Oh, yeah, the food here is disgusting! *There is a fibroid tumor here the size of a lemon. It presses against us and positions itself on your womb. Of course, you don't feel it, though. There is too much debris and clutter in the way for you to even notice what we're going through.*

I'm writing to you with hopes that this message is not infiltrated by Anger or Rage or whatever her name is.

By the way, I thought you'd like to know that in the cell directly above mine are your inner children. They, too, are treated horribly. They, too, want out.

142

We are waiting on you, Beloved. You are the only one who can release the shackles. You are the light we've been waiting for.

We're depending on you, Robin.

Free us! Free Yourself!

Lovingly,

Power Within

Dear Body....

Dear Body,

I am writing this letter to let you know that you might begin to experience some shifts in the way you feel. I'd like to thank you for all you are and have been to me. I apologize for those times I abused, misused, or was confused about what you represent to and for me.

This is the opportune time to let you know that I heard you, and I hear you! I hear you when you cry for rest. I hear you when you yearn to be caressed. I hear you when you tell me you've had enough, and I apologize for ignoring you in the past. Forgive me for putting the weight of my thoughts, fears, and emotions on you. Forgive me for believing that I was unloved, unloving, and unlovable. Forgive me for neglecting to nurture you, protect you, and for using you as the fortress of my protection. Forgive me for stretching and molding you as the embodiment of unforgiveness and anger.

I now understand, acknowledge, and accept the powerful gift of forgiveness. I realize that F.O.R.G.I.V.E.N.E.S.S.™ is for me first. It is a conscious state of being that is to be Free of Rage, Guilt, Illness, Victimhood, Envy, Negative Ego & Self-Sabotage.

Through the powerful gift of forgiveness, I free myself from the self-created illusion of victimhood. It allows me to release and move through suppressed and repressed anger. Forgiveness erases guilt, shame, and self-loathing, and it pulls the shackles of unworthiness off, one by one, allowing my heart to beat, my lungs to breathe, and my skin to radiate. Body, forgiveness allows me to redefine you as my temple, rather than my fortress. I'm clear about that now.

I am learning to be compassionate with myself as I align in mind, body, and spirit. I'm moving to a place of intimacy and self-acceptance. I have cursed you for so long, and now, it is taking time for me to reprogram the self-limiting, self-degrading thoughts I've held and projected onto you.

I'm really getting excited because my prayers are being answered. God is really supporting me and ushering me to accept my greatness and my anointing. There's so much support available to me now. Who knew that my one word prayer, "Help" would produce such an amazing outcome?

The best is yet to come. While there's still work to do, both inner and outer, I created a vision board... just for you! I call it, "Loving the Me I See." I've envisioned alignment and healing of mind, body, and spirit and emotional integrity. I think it's everything

145

you've ever wanted! There are symbolic pictures of me loving you, touching you, and nurturing you. In each image, I am grinning from ear to ear, expressing joy and gratitude. In these images, you are light and healthy. There are images of movement, Body! You've always wanted that. I'm feeding you healthy foods that foster Perfect Health.

Wait... are you ready? Oh, I'm so excited! I heard Spirit speak to me! Spirit said, "Be Clear. Ask for, and then create what you desire." I focused on my desires. I integrated all five of my senses to call it forward. It was challenging at first, but then I closed my eyes, and I went inside. I allowed myself to go there and experience it all, Body! I experienced and expressed true intimacy and self-love. I experienced myself loving myself unconditionally. I experienced and expressed forgiveness and compassion for others and myself. I saw and felt myself free, healed, whole, and healthy. I basked in the experience of love, light, and peace flowing in, through, and as me. I saw brilliant colors such as Red, Orange, Yellow, Green, Blue, Violet, and White. I then realized that my energy centers were aligned. My mind, body, and spirit were aligned! It felt like a ReBirth. I wanted to be there forever.

While basking in that moment, I saw him standing on the side. He was without a face, but I saw him! He was built. Deep chocolate, tight abs, juicy

146

*butt, straight white teeth... and those shoulders...
Whew!*

*It wasn't just the noticeable, either. He seemed
different. It was something about his ways of being. I
saw white light shine his way and knew that God was
nudging me to invite him into the sacred space (what I
was calling forth in my heart and mind). I was a little
hesitant, but I chose to trust God. I invited him into
the vision. He was powerful, loving, authentic,
responsible, compassionate, and vulnerable.*

*There was no conversation. I just trusted that I
attracted my reflection. I used my senses again...
seeing us on romantic dates. We laughed, played,
kissed, talked, and enjoyed each other's company. He
romanced my mind with his intellect, and I felt safe to
be with him. He's really diggin' you, Body! I imagined
us joyful, empowered, and inspired as we grew
together in heart and soul.*

*Whew! Did you feel that, Body? Did you see it?
Well, guess what? If you didn't, I have the visual for us
to call forth day-by-day, hour by hour, and moment by
moment. I'll leave it up next to my other vision boards
near the altar so we can bask in Truth and expectancy
as we lean on Spirit for guidance and direction. I'm so
excited!*

*Love, Light & Peace
Robin*

The Crossover

I'm crossing over into a state of **Conscious Living.**
*I am releasing the stories, people, and feelings that
kept me on the other side. It's beautiful on this side,
and the glory of the crossing is the victory in seeing
through a new lens.*
*My perception has changed because my perspective
has changed.*
*My thinking is the direct reflection of the Most High
God as I honor and abide by the Law of Mind Action.*

*I acknowledge that what I think about comes about.
On this side, I accept the call.
I see and map out the vision.*

I am crossing over into a state of **Forgiveness.**
*I am healing on a deeper level because I've opened my
heart; my mind is free of clutter, and my body is
cleansing.*
*Love flows in through and as me as I forgive the stories
of my past.*
*I acknowledge that I am not my circumstance.
I accept that all that has taken place in my life was
predestined to bring me to this moment.*

I am crossing over into a state of **Gratitude.**
*I'm thankful for the human vessels of love who
supported me in acknowledging that LOVE is the
language of the Most High God.*

On this side, there is no blame.
There is inner-standing.
I inner-stand my response-ability.
I have the ability to respond.
I inner-stand my soul's mission—the purpose of my
existence.
I am fearfully and wonderfully made in the image and
likeness of the Most High God.

I express my femininity in many ways and give praise
to the Divine Mother, for without her, I would not
know how to Be.
I trust myself in all I do because I now trust that I am
surrounded and guided by ancestors, spiritual guides,
and angels.

I have the courage to be myself because I finally accept
that I am worthy!
I appreciate myself in all I do because my intention is
to serve by educating, empowering, and facilitating
healing in all I do. I am responsible for my words,
behaviors, and actions.

I accept myself as healer, teacher, mother, friend.
I accept myself as Me! I honor myself for taking the
necessary steps to look within and empowering myself
to push through uncomfortable feelings to be an
example of self-love, forgiveness, truth, hope, and
healing for others.

149

I know myself as the Beloved daughter in whom God is well pleased.

I am crossing over, yet my rite of passage is just beginning.
I have yet to fulfill my destiny.
I am ready.
I am healed, whole, and healthy.
The gifts of the Universe are available to me.
I need only ask.
I am ready to take TheRiteStep into my future with wisdom from my past.

I am crossing over into a conscious state of
Dedicated Service.
I am sharing the good news, supporting others in moving through, and inner-standing with power, purpose, and passion.

*I am crossing over into my very own **ReBirth!***
I am awakening from the illusion of self-doubt and rewriting the script of my life.

I am crossing over.

Meet me on the other side.

About the Author

Robin St. Clair is an Empowerment Strategist, Intuitive Counselor, and Certified Reiki Master/Teacher, who has dedicated her life to educating, empowering, and facilitating healing in herself and others.

Robin received personal development and coaching training from Inner Visions Institute for Spiritual Development and Momentum Education, and she is committed to living out loud and *on purpose*, while answering *"the call"* for her life.

After completing intense study and several years of an introspective healing journey, Robin birthed TheRiteStep as a reminder of the healing power of Sankofa, which teaches that we must reach back and gather the best of what our past has taught us. We must do this so we can achieve our full potential, thus taking the *right step* into the future with wisdom from the past.

In her work, Robin combines twenty-four years of labor relations experience and eight years of personal development and coaching, affording her an outstanding foundation as an effective communicator and an empowerment facilitator.

To learn more about Robin St. Clair, upcoming books or TheRiteStep programs and events, please visit www.theritestep.com.

Made in the USA
Charleston, SC
16 March 2014